FRUITS
AND
VEGETABLES

1001 Gardening Questions Answered

by
The Editors of Garden Way Publishing
Foreword by Louise Riotte

A GARDEN WAY PUBLISHING BOOK

STOREY COMMUNICATIONS, INC.
POWNAL, VERMONT 05261

Produced by Storey Communications, Inc.
President, M. John Storey
Executive Vice President of Administration, Martha M. Storey
Publisher, Thomas Woll

Written by Jeff Silva and the Editors of Garden Way Publishing
Cover and interior design by Andrea Gray
Edited by Gwen W. Steege
Illustrated by Alison Kolesar, except insect drawings, pages
    18-19, 86-87, and 89, by Judy Eliason
Production by Andrea Gray and Rebecca Babbitt
Front and back cover photographs by Positive Images,
    Jerry Howard
Interior photographs by Maggie Oster, Photo/Nats (Dorothy S.
    Long), Positive Images (Tad Goodale, Margaret Hensel, Jerry
    Howard, Ivan Massar), Ann Reilly, Stark Brothers Nurseries and
    Orchards, Martha M. Storey, and Ron West
Chapter opening photographs by Ron West (1), Maggie Oster (2),
    Positive Images (Tad Goodale, 3; Jerry Howard, 5), and Ann Reilly
    (4, 6).
Map by Northern Cartographic
Typesetting by StereoType & Design, So. Burlington, VT.

Quality Printing and Binding By:
ARCATA GRAPHICS/KINGSPORT
Press and Roller Streets
Kingsport, TN 37662 U.S.A.

Fruits and vegetables: 1001 gardening questions answered / by the editors of Garden
Way Publishing; foreword by Louise Riotte.
    "A Garden Way Publishing book."
    Includes bibliographical references (p. 148).
    ISBN 0-88266-571-5: $16.95
    1. Fruit-culture—Miscellanea.   2. Vegetable gardening-
—Miscellanea.   I. Garden Way Publishing.
SB355.F785   1990
635-dc20   89-84636
                                                                      CIP

Contents

As delightful as any kind of gardening is, raising fresh, homegrown fruits and vegetables is particularly enriching. Sun-ripened tomatoes; golden ears of corn; tender beans and peas; bright, succulent squashes; perfect heads of broccoli and cauliflower; crisp, flavorful apples; tangy-sweet berries; and as much lettuce, cabbage, and radishes as you can eat—these are, perhaps, reward enough, but growing your own fruits and vegetables can bring other benefits as well.

First of all, when they are harvested at their peak, home-grown fruits and vegetables far surpass in nutritional value those ordinarily found at the supermarket. In addition, the very process of gardening helps promote good health and well-being. It is good exercise and a uniquely beneficial mental therapy that can be enjoyed by young and old alike. After a day spent trying to solve problems and to cope with the tensions of work, time spent in the open air performing simple garden chores offers a change of pace and an excellent way to unwind.

More subtly, growing your own fruits and vegetables can help satisfy certain creative instincts: You can thrill with a sense of achievement as you watch your efforts result in the vigorous growth and development of plants laden for harvest. What gardener, biting into a juicy peach or a sweet-tasting ear of corn, is not convinced that what he or she has grown is better tasting than anything else ever eaten?

Another, more tangible benefit is that in good years, you will most likely raise more of your fruits and vegetables than you can ever use. That gives you a delightful opportunity to share with friends and neighbors, or even to donate your extra produce to agencies that provide food for the needy.

Although certain factors, such as climate and lack of space, may appear as obstacles to beginning gardeners, they needn't be. Consider that today, more than ever before, you can protect your plants by using polyethylene covers and other season-stretching techniques. If you have space constraints, you will find that many fruits and vegetables thrive in pots outdoors or even under fluorescent lighting indoors. Are you rushed for time? All forms of gardening do require a certain amount of time and devotion, but if you enjoy the hobby of gardening, the time it requires will not seem excessive. Concerned about cost? Seeds and plants are still one of the best bargains around, with dozens of catalogs to peruse for your favorites, or you may enjoy trading seeds and plants with friends and neighbors. And, of course, in the long run, you will save money by producing your own food.

If you are a new or a more experienced gardener, whether or not you've been successful in the past, you probably still need to seek occasional professional advice. With so many gardening books on the market, it's exciting when a book like *Fruits and Vegetables: 1001 Gardening Questions Answered* shows us that the subject of gardening has barely been touched—that there are many new and adventurous paths to be explored.

Louise Riotte
Author, *Carrots Love Tomatoes*

Martha Storey

1 *Your Home Fruit Orchard*

Abundant, fresh fruit for baking, jams and jellies, or simply eating fresh from the harvest is surprisingly easy for home gardeners to grow. Even for those with limited space, container-grown dwarf trees or hanging strawberry baskets will provide an impressive amount of fruit with relatively little care. And fruit trees and bushes are often extremely ornamental additions to the home landscape throughout the season. The brilliant pink spring blossoms of a peach or the fall-ripened orange fruits of a leafless persimmon make a stunning addition to a front yard or back patio. If you have room for a garden of any size, you have room to grow fruit.

CLIMATE CONSIDERATIONS

Knowing certain details about the climate where you live is even more important when you are planning to grow fruit than it is for vegetables or flowers. Not only do temperate climate fruits need a certain amount of warm weather, but they also require a certain amount of cold weather—called the *chilling requirement* (see page 2). To determine which fruits you can grow where you live, study the descriptions of individual plants on pages 23-51, ask your county Extension Service agent for advice about what varieties are suited to your region, and search for a dependable local or mail-order nursery that carries the full range of fruit-bearing plants that grow well in your area.

What are hardiness zones?

These zones (see map, page 149), established by the United States Department of Agriculture, are numbered 1 through 10:

◀ *The brilliant pink blossoms of a peach tree make a stunning addition to the spring landscape.*

Zone 1 receives the lowest average annual minimum temperature; Zone 10 receives the highest. The zones don't necessarily separate the best from the worst gardening places. Furthermore, even if your area has temperatures that dip very low in winter, it may have a greater number of frost-free days or the sun may shine more often than in areas with milder winter temperatures.

Is it true that some varieties of peaches, apricots, and blueberries will grow in much colder regions than commonly considered possible for these fruits?

Yes. By hybridizing, plant breeders have developed strains of fruits that can withstand colder than usual climates. You should, however, approach such varieties with caution, planting only one or two, until you are sure they will stand up to conditions in your yard. The *length* of your area's growing season is just as critical as its annual minimum temperature. A number of other climatic factors should be considered as well: Extremes of wind, rain, snow, or ice can be even more devastating than very cold winters. Early spring thaws in cold-weather regions can bring on early blossoming in apricots; subsequent cold snaps will kill the blossoms and ruin the crop. Wet springs harm peaches by spreading leaf curl.

Is there any reason why I shouldn't plant all extra-hardy varieties, just in case a rare cold winter comes along?

Before you do that, consider the fact that extra hardiness often comes at the sacrifice of flavor, disease resistance, and other virtues. Decide whether this trade-off is worthwhile to you, as well as whether these extra-hardy varieties will grow in your climate at all.

Exactly what is a chilling requirement?

The fruiting period must be followed by a dormant period during which the plant rests and regains strength for another fruit set the following year. The length of this dormant period is measured in hours between 32° and 45° F. Varieties with low winter chilling requirements need from 300 to 400 hours below 45° F.; medium chilling needs are 400 to 700 hours; high chilling needs are 700 to 1,000 hours.

Can I extend the warm season for growing fruits?

Yes, but with difficulty. You can sometimes find a microclimate within the boundaries of your own land where, because of the amount of available sun or the slope of the land, you can grow plants that would find a spot just a few feet away inhospitable. You can grow trees against walls, under plastic tunnels, or in greenhouses, and you can even cover dwarf trees with cloth draped over a wooden frame and warm them from below with light bulbs or candles. This sort of troublesome protection is not practical year after year with a number of plantings. It's better to plant the proper varieties for your region.

Can I extend the winter chill in my area?

Aside from planting in the coldest section of your yard—for example, at the bottom of a slope where cold air runs at night—there is nothing practical you can do.

Will fruits and berries grow in the shade?

All fruits must have full exposure to the sun for most of the day. Although they will grow in partial shade, the harvest will be light and the fruit not as sweet. Sour cherries need less sun than other tree fruits.

How important to fruits, berries, and grapes is soil drainage?

A well-drained site is very important. Peach and cherry trees are less tolerant of soggy soils than are apples and pears, but no fruit tree will grow in soil that is always wet.

EVALUATING YOUR SITE

•

Most fruit trees have a chilling requirement—a dormant period measured in hours when temperatures range between 32° and 45°F. The chilling requirement for this Rainier cherry tree is 700 hours.

Stark Brothers Nurseries and Orchards

I would like to plant a peach tree in the center of my vegetable garden. Is this a wise thing to do?

If the tree will need to be sprayed for pest and disease control (see pages 18-20), this may not be the best place for it, as you must never allow fruit tree sprays to drift onto vegetables or fruits. Fig and persimmon trees, which need no spraying, might be appropriate for such settings. If your garden space is limited, however, even small trees may take up more room and cast more shade than would be desirable for the vegetables you are trying to grow.

Can I plant grapevines, berry bushes, and fruit trees on sloping ground?

Midway down gentle slopes is ideal, because cold air will drain away from plantings on frosty nights. Low spots surrounded by higher land are the least desirable, because cold air drains into them.

What sort of soil is best for fruits?

Most fruits grow best in the same sort of soil that is good for growing vegetables (see pages 60-61).

Are there any kinds of fruits that will grow on land that is too poor for garden vegetables?

Figs do best without supplemental nitrogen and prefer heavy clay soil, so you might consider them if your climate is suitable. Grapes will thrive on soils containing clay, slate, gravel, and sand, although the better choice for them is a well-drained, deep, fertile loam. In general, it is best to improve a poor soil before planting fruit in it. (See pages 61-67 for methods of improving soil.)

Will fruit trees grow in thin soil over a layer of rock?

If you have less covering than 12 inches, no fruit trees will survive, and you should consider planting genetic dwarf fruit trees in large tubs instead.

We live on the seacoast and get steady winds during most of the year. Will fruits grow well here?

Wind is a problem for most plants, because it dries out plant tissue and physically damages limbs and branches. Build or plant windbreaks, behind which you can plant dwarf trees. Consult your local Extension Service agent, who will give you advice about windbreaks based on the experience of others in your area.

There is no plant nursery in my area. Where can I get good planting stock?

Choose a respectable, well-established mail-order nursery, such as the ones listed at the back of this book. Be sure to plant stock promptly upon its arrival.

How reliable are the berry bushes and fruit trees I see for sale at grocery and drug stores?

Too often such places sell plants that are not suited to the local climate. If you see a healthy-looking specimen of a variety you know will grow well under local conditions (see Chapter 3 for specific varieties), you might try it, but check closely for damage, pests, and disease before you buy. Remember, too, that the sellers may not be able to answer the questions that arise as the specimen grows.

Does it matter where the stock I buy was grown?

No. Named varieties are genetically identical and will perform identically in your garden no matter where they were produced.

I have heard that I must plant two of each kind of fruit tree I grow. Is that true?

Sometimes, but not always. Before you purchase a fruit tree, you will need to know whether it will produce fruit on its own, or whether it needs to grow near a pollinator tree of a different variety. Trees that pollinate themselves are called *self-fruitful*; trees that cannot pollinate themselves—which include most fruit trees—are called *self-sterile*. The descriptions of individual fruits in Chapter 3 tell which ones need a pollinator and which can stand alone. Self-sterile trees not only need a pollinator tree within 100 feet of them, but that pollinator tree must blossom at approximately the same time or it will not fertilize its neighbor. Because bees carry the pollen from one tree to another, it is important to avoid the use of any substance on your property that might kill bees.

Could you please explain the difference between container-grown, balled-and-burlapped, and bare-rooted plants?

Container-grown plants have been grown in some kind of pot—usually peat, plastic, or clay—for most or all of their lives. They should be kept moist, in a semishaded spot, until you are ready to plant them. Balled-and-burlapped plants have been dug up with the soil carefully maintained around their roots and wrapped in burlap (or plastic-backed burlap). Bare-rooted plants, too, have been dug from their growing place, but without retaining the root ball. If you get your plants from a mail-order nursery, they will most likely come bare-rooted, with their roots protected with something like damp sphagnum moss. Bare-rooted plants are the most susceptible to damage.

Bees, which carry pollen from one flowering fruit tree to another, are valuable assets to fruit growers.

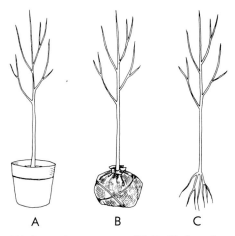

A   B   C

(A) Container-grown. (B) Balled-and-burlapped. (C) Bare-rooted.

The roots of bare-rooted trees should be submerged in water for from 3 to 24 hours before planting.

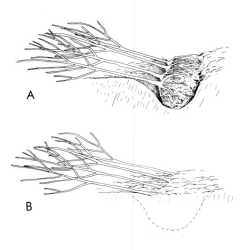

If it will be more than 24 hours before you can plant a tree in its permanent location, heel it in by (A) laying it on its side in a shallow trench and (B) covering the roots with at least 6 inches of soil. Water the trees lightly and keep them shaded.

Are there any advantages to planting bare-rooted plants?

Bare-rooted plants are almost always considerably cheaper than potted or balled-and-burlapped plants, and your first harvest is not likely to come any later. In cold-winter areas, bare-rooted plants should be planted in the spring, so if you live up north and want to put in fruit during the summer, you should buy potted or balled plants.

What should I do with my plants when I get them home?

Immediately remove bare-rooted plants from the protective material in which they are enclosed. Submerge the roots in water. You can leave them in water for up to twenty-four hours in a garage or shaded, protected place. Plant them as soon as weather permits. A good nursery won't ship your plants to you until the proper planting time where you live. Wrap the roots of balled plants in plastic and keep them, too, in a sheltered location. If you must hold either bare-rooted or balled-and-burlapped stock for more than twenty-four hours, plant them temporarily using a technique known as *heeling in* (see illustration).

What size fruit tree should I buy?

Buy trees on the small side, but not tiny little whips. Small trees will establish themselves sooner than larger, older trees with larger root systems. Whether the tree you plant is simply one long stem or is lightly branched does not make a great amount of difference.

What other things should I consider when choosing among varieties?

Be practical and take into account your desires and needs. What kind of fruit do you like to eat? How much space do you have? What is your climate like? Do you can, freeze, or dry fruits? Choose varieties suited to your purposes.

Do dwarf fruit trees have any special advantages?

Full-sized fruit can be produced on the diminutive, attractive dwarf fruit trees that are now widely available in increasingly many different varieties. These trees produce roughly the same amount of fruit—or sometimes more—for the amount of space they take up as standard-sized trees, and usually at a younger age. Pruning, spraying, and harvesting dwarf trees is easier, too, as you need have no tall ladders or special equipment. In fact, they need less pruning because they are not as vigorous growers.

What are the disadvantages of dwarf trees?

They require more frequent irrigating in dry climates than do standard trees. Some are not as sturdy in high winds and need

These dwarf apple trees are easier to prune, spray, and harvest than standard-size apple trees—and they bear a surprising amount of fruit.

more support when their limbs are heavy with fruit. They usually don't live as long as standard trees, nor are they as hardy against cold. Deep, icy snow may break off low-growing branches, and herbivorous animals can easily reach foliage.

What are genetic dwarfs?

Genetic dwarfs are the smallest fruit trees of all. Though they grow well in large tubs, they can also be planted in the ground, where they will reach a larger size—some of them up to 8 or 9 feet. If you live in the North, you can grow genetic dwarfs in tubs. Take them into an unheated shelter (*not* the heated house) during the winter months. Genetic dwarfs bear fruit of medium size that, while generally not of as high a quality as the larger trees, is still tasty. They usually come into bearing the second year after being planted.

What are five-in-one trees, and are they worth considering?

These curious trees consist of a rootstock with five different varieties of the same fruit—usually apples—grafted to it. These trees are rather expensive, and not as easy to grow as one might think. Often one or two of the grafted varieties will grow much more vigorously than the others, and need more pruning. In addition, very careful attention must be taken to avoid entirely cutting off one of the varieties during the dormant pruning season, when it is hardest to distinguish one variety from another. On the other hand, the trees can be quite beautiful if they bloom in multicolor, and their novelty appeals to many.

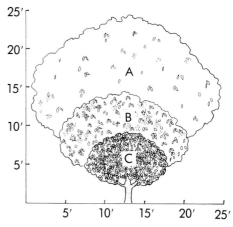

(A) Standard. (B) Semi-dwarf. (C) Dwarf.

7

2 Planting and Growing Fruits and Berries

Growing fruits is surprisingly easy—aside from annual pruning and an intelligent program of pest and disease control, there is little of the day-to-day care required by some vegetables and flowers. In addition, many fruits are little affected by moderate fluctuations in weather. If you follow the given here on planting, fertilizing, watering, and pruning your trees and bushes, you will soon be harvesting succulent fruits for your table and pantry. Be sure to prepare your soil, assemble the planting and staking materials that you will need, and even dig your holes before your planting stock arrives.

How should I prepare the soil before planting fruits and berries?

Incorporate about ½ bushel of compost or aged manure per planting hole to lighten a heavy soil or improve the water-holding ability of a sandy soil. This is best done in the fall for a spring planting, but always *before* your stock arrives. A green manure crop (see page 61) will also improve the soil before planting. Refer to pages 60-67 for other ways to improve your soil.

Rather than trying to improve all the soil in the area, can't I improve just the spots where my fruit trees will be?

Although your trees, properly spaced, will use all the soil in the area when they are mature, you can start out by preparing the soil just in a 5-foot circle around the planting holes. You can then continue to improve the surrounding soil as your trees

◀ *If espaliered, apples are among the many fruits that can be grown in limited space.*

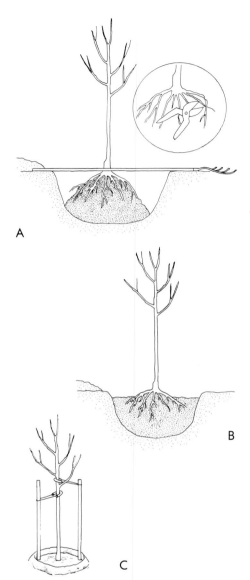

To plant a bare-rooted tree, (A) in a hole twice the width of the plant's root spread, mound up soil at the bottom, dampen it, and set the tree roots on it so that the graft union lines up at 3 or 4 inches above ground level; cut off any withered or broken roots. (B) Fill the hole, gently pressing down on the soil with your hands as you go and taking care to leave no air pockets around roots; mound soil around the tree about 3 inches above ground level, leaving the graft union 1 inch above ground level; water well. (C) Create a shallow, doughnut-shaped dish in the soil around the tree; drive two stakes into the ground on either side of the tree and stretch wires from the stakes to the tree, covering the wires with hose where they touch the tree.

grow by planting green manure crops and adding manure and compost as necessary. (See page 61 and information on specific trees.)

How early in the spring should fruit trees and grapes be planted?

Plant just as early as the soil can be worked. As long as the trees or vines are dormant, there is no danger of planting too early, provided the soil has dried out enough to be worked. Avoid working clay soils that are wet enough to be squeezed into a tight, elastic mass (see page 63). In warm-winter areas, bare-rooted plants can be planted in autumn, when leaves have just begun to fall.

How far apart should I space fruit trees?

That depends entirely on the mature size of the trees you are planting. Fruit trees usually grow about as wide as they do tall, so determine the mature height of the varieties you are planting, and space the young trees so that at full size their outer branches will come just short of touching the branches of the next tree over.

How can I know whether my trees need to be staked when I plant them, and how should I go about staking them?

Stake dwarf trees, trees liable to encounter high winds or physical abuse from animals or passersby, or trees 4 feet or taller. Sink two stakes into the ground, one on each side of the tree, just outside of where the roots are, and *loosely* tie the tree to them with rags, rubber strips, old nylon stockings, or nonsticky plastic tape—don't use strong, thin string, or anything that might cut into the bark. If your tree is quite small at planting time, but you expect to stake it as it grows, put the stakes in now, when there is less risk of damaging the roots.

Should I prune my trees at planting time?

Container-grown trees that have been in their pots for some time should be pruned only very lightly by removing just broken or poorly placed growth. To encourage strong root growth, cut back the tops of bare-rooted or balled-and-burlapped trees by about one half, or slightly more if the trees are especially tall and skinny. You can either remove all the side (scaffold) branches or cut them back by half.

How should balled-and-burlapped trees be planted?

Follow the procedure used for bare-rooted trees (see illustration). When you lower the root ball onto the mound of soil in your hole, pull the burlap covering away from the tops and sides (but not from the bottom) before filling the hole with soil. If the covering is plastic, remove it from the hole. Remember to apply plenty of water as you go, as well as when you're finished.

How should I plant container-grown trees?

Plant them as you would bare-rooted trees, but don't attempt to break the roots free from the tight ball of soil they hold. Loosen the outer roots from the soil ball by rubbing them with your fingers, roughing them up with a stick, or spraying them with a stream of water. If, on the other hand, the tree hasn't been growing in the container long and the soil falls away when you lift the plant from the container, shake the dirt free and treat as a bare-rooted tree.

When should I begin fertilizing newly planted fruit trees?

There are no hard and fast rules about fertilizing. If a young tree is growing well, looking healthy, and producing good crops, the only fertilizer it may need is a nitrogen supplement. Large, mature trees usually need 1 pound of nitrogen per year; smaller, immature trees, from ¼ to ⅓ of a pound per year. Keep the ground around the trees mulched with an organic material that will decompose into the soil. Leave a ring of exposed soil 8 inches around the trunk, to discourage rodents and insects. In addition to contributing nutrients to the soil, mulch will keep down weeds, prevent water evaporation during dry weather, prevent erosion, and ameliorate soil temperature fluctuations.

Should I add phosphorus and potassium to the soil, too?

Most soils contain enough of these nutrients for growing fruit trees. If a soil test shows otherwise, or your local Extension Service advises you to, add them before planting, and subsequently as further tests dictate.

At what time of year should I fertilize?

Early spring, after the trees have leafed out, is best. In general, the least desirable time to fertilize is just before, or during, fruit growth. Fast-acting, commercial fertilizers should go down in early spring. Bulky organic fertilizers, because they release nutrients slowly, can be added later in the season (though not just before winter), and pose a lesser risk of overfertilization. In colder areas, do not fertilize after the first half of summer, because this encourages late, tender new growth that would be susceptible to winter damage. To fertilize, pull back the mulch and give a light application of a high-nitrogen fertilizer, or a 2- to 3-inch layer of steer manure, dusted around the drip line (corresponding to the outermost branches) and then turned into the top few inches of soil. Water thoroughly. Don't cultivate too deeply or you might injure the roots.

Will a cover crop help my fruits and berries?

A cover crop of clover or some other legume will provide a living mulch and contribute nitrogen to the soil as well. Flower-

FERTILIZING FRUIT TREES

ing cover crops such as mustard, clover, buckwheat, and sweet alyssum attract bees and other beneficial insects. Cover crops should be mowed occasionally, and their clippings left to decompose into the soil.

What sort of pH do fruit trees need?

A slightly acid soil is ideal, but not absolutely necessary. Severely imbalanced soils should be corrected.

WATERING FRUIT TREES

A drip watering system takes water to the exact spot where it is needed.

How much water does a newly planted fruit tree need?

Keep a watch on your tree for the entire first year, and water heavily once a week when it doesn't rain. In a heavy soil, too much water will flood the soil, robbing plants of oxygen, and in a sandy soil too much water will wash away valuable nutrients. Mulch the soil to conserve moisture.

How can I know when my fruit trees need to be watered?

Water mature trees when the soil is dry 4 to 6 inches below the surface. If the leaves are wilted early in the day, you've allowed them to get too dry. Water deeply and not often, adjusting your watering schedule to the weather rather than the calendar. If the ground beneath your trees is always moist, you're watering too often. Keep the root crown dry.

What is the best way to water?

Although it involves a substantial initial investment, a drip watering system will later save you money on water, for it puts water only where your trees need it. On dry, sloping ground it is almost a must because water loss from runoff is eliminated. Disadvantages include not being able to grow green manure or cover crops and the trouble of working around drip lines when adding bulky soil amendments. Drip watering is probably not worth the expense with standard trees that need little irrigation, but for dwarf trees it is superior. Try to keep the ground adjacent to the trunks dry.

Do I need to water a fruit tree growing in a lawn that gets watered twice a week?

Yes, because the relatively shallow watering most lawns receive is not adequate for fruit trees. Use a deep root irrigator to water trees growing in lawns. This tool, available at any garden center or nursery, is a long, hollow needle that attaches to your garden hose and applies water slowly to the soil down where a tree's roots are.

Is pruning fruit trees and berries really essential?

Yes, and proper pruning is quickly learned and easy to do. Fruit trees need pruning into a shape that will invite sunlight into their interior branches, that will allow good air circulation and ease of spraying and harvesting, and that will create sturdy limbs that can support a heavy load of ripening fruit. The trees also need to be pruned to remove dead and diseased wood. For information on how to prune grapes and berries, see individual entries in Chapter 3.

Is there one principle to keep in mind that will help me as I get started pruning?

Err on the side of pruning too little: No serious harm will come to your trees if you leave a little too much wood on them. You can always remove it later when you are more sure of what you are doing.

At what time of year should I prune?

Prune during the dormant season, before buds have begun to swell. As the tree puts out new growth in the spring, you can pinch off long or unwanted shoots, but it's best to refrain from major pruning during the time when a tree is actively growing.

In what shape should I train my trees to grow?

Refer to the individual fruit tree descriptions in Chapter 3 for the shape best suited to the trees you are growing. Fruit trees are most often pruned in one of three configurations—open-center (also called vase training), modified leader, or central leader.

Open-center training does not create as strong a limb structure as other methods, a potentially serious problem if the tree will carry heavy weights of fruit, as well as of ice and snow. It also needs more lateral space than trees pruned in other ways. It has the advantage, however, of letting sunlight into a tree's center, where the light and warmth ripen the fruit and dry up moist, potentially disease-causing conditions. Open-center-trained trees are easiest to keep from growing too tall.

Modified-leader-trained trees are sturdier than open-center-trained trees, because they don't carry their load of fruit (or snow or ice) so far away from their trunk. Modified-leader-trained trees have a single trunk that runs a few feet higher than the trunk of an open-center-trained tree, and then branches out. Trees grow to a moderate height this way.

Central-leader-trained trees are the strongest and tallest of the three configurations. A single trunk continues up the center of the tree, with all scaffold branches emanating from it. Trees trained in this way are difficult to prune, spray, thin, and harvest, and are hard to drape with protective netting if birds are

PRUNING FRUIT TREES

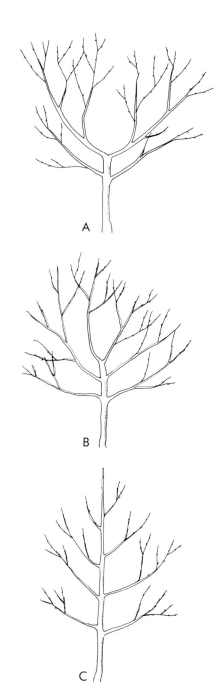

(A) Open-center- or vase-trained.
(B) Modified-leader-trained.
(C) Central-leader-trained.

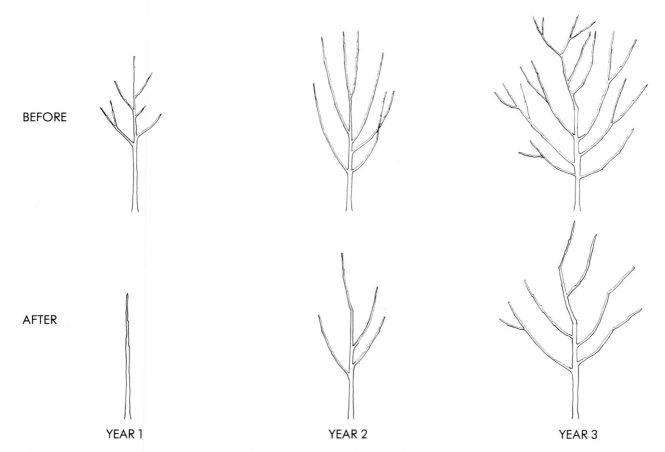

BEFORE

AFTER

YEAR 1   YEAR 2   YEAR 3

Characteristic pruning during the first three years of a tree's growth.

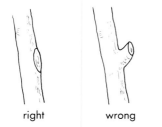

right   wrong

When pruning side branches, leave no stub.

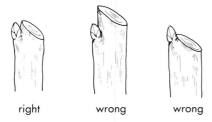

right   wrong   wrong

Avoid making pruning cuts too close or too far from a bud.

a problem. On the other hand, they serve as windbreaks, offer privacy and shade, and are quite stately and lovely.

How often should I prune?

Prune your trees when you plant them, and then yearly thereafter.

How should I prune for the sake of maintenance?

Remove any diseased, broken, or dead wood, and cover the cuts with tree-patching compound if they are 2 inches or more across. Prune off lateral branches that extend so far horizontally that they are likely to break under heavy loads. Remove tangled wood and excessive growth that blocks sunlight.

How can I prune to bring an old neglected tree back into shape?

Go easy on the old-timers. Take away a small amount of wood each season until, within three to five years, the tree has the amount of wood you want on it. You can't very well train an old tree into a new shape, but you can prune it to take advantage of the shape in which it has been growing over the years.

Are there any advantages to espaliering, or is it done solely for ornamental purposes?

To espalier fruit trees means to train them to grow flat. Their great advantage is that they can be grown in a quite small place up against a wall, and they will thrive even if their roots are underneath paved walks or driveways. Since many fruit trees need to be planted in pairs (see page 5), two single-stem cordon espaliers (see illustration) can be planted two feet apart, providing pollen for each other, yet taking up little space. If you plant an espalier against a white-painted, south-facing wall, you may be able to grow a variety that normally needs warmer climates. And they are easy to access for care and harvest.

What are the disadvantages of growing espaliers?

If you buy them already trained, they are expensive. Although it is not hard to train them yourself, you must prune them continuously throughout the growing season or they will lose their shape. Preventive spraying can stain the structure against which the espalier is grown, and painting the structure is difficult.

Do espaliers encounter any problems that other fruit trees do not?

Since their trunks are not shaded by their leaves, they can get burned by the sun. To counter this, paint the trunks white. In warmer climates, espaliers planted against a wall can get too hot: Temperatures above 90° F. will damage the leaves and fruit. If this might be a problem where you live, plant them against an east wall, along a free-standing wire system stretched between posts, or in some other place that does not receive direct sun in the heat of the day.

What fruit trees are best for espaliering?

Any tree that you can get on dwarf rootstock will work. Apples, cherries, peaches, pears, and figs are among the best for espalier.

ESPALIERS

•

A single-stem cordon espalier.

To train a single-stem cordon espalier, (A) plant tree midway between concrete-based posts in front of tautly stretched wires. (B) With strips of cloth, tie two side shoots to the lowest wire, leaving a third shoot to grow as the trunk. (C) During the second spring of growth, train two more side shoots to the second wire; leave a shoot to continue trunk growth.

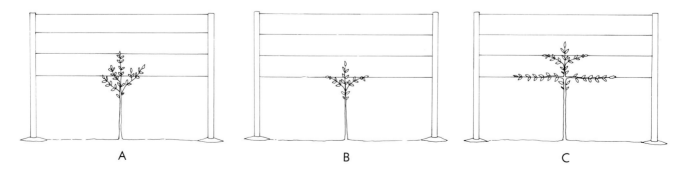

A   B   C

How should I feed and water espaliers?

Apply a small handful of a high-nitrogen fertilizer to espaliers in the spring, and then prune them back heavily in the summer. Water thoroughly after fertilizing.

GROWING FRUIT TREES IN CONTAINERS

·

To repot a container-grown tree, gently remove the plant from the pot (soil should be damp, but not wet); cut away an inch of soil and roots around the circumference of the root ball; wash the container with soap and hot water; spread new soil on the bottom of the pot; center the plant in the pot, packing new soil around the sides; water thoroughly; prune lightly, if necessary.

Can I grow all kinds of fruit trees in containers?

Yes, though all but fig trees must be dwarfs.

What sort of container should I use?

Anything that is well drained and large enough to hold the tree's roots. Make sure that your containers are not treated with any toxic chemical. (For further information about container plants, see pages 83-85.)

What are your suggestions for watering container-grown fruits?

Water often, especially during dry weather. Water in such a way that you don't disturb the soil with a hard stream. Drip systems work well with container-grown fruit trees. Mulch to conserve water.

What is the best way to fertilize container-grown fruits?

Liquid fertilizers, such as fish emulsion, are ideal. Fertilize more often than you would in-ground plants—about once a month—but with about one-half the strength recommended for in-ground plants. Fertilizer is quickly washed out of container-grown plants because of frequent watering, but they can't withstand heavy doses or they'll get burned.

How often should I repot container-grown fruit trees?

If after a few years in the same pot, a plant starts sending roots up to the soil surface, seems to need watering too often, or simply lacks vigor, the tree is giving signals that it needs repotting.

Can I grow fruit trees completely indoors?

This is possible, but most need full sun to produce good fruit. Try growing trees outdoors and bringing them inside for brief spells when they are at their most beautiful.

Where should I store a plant while it is being protected from winter cold?

An unheated garage is a good place to keep a tree during its dormancy. The temperature must stay above 15° F.

Is it okay to shake fruit out of a tree onto a blanket?

You're likely to bruise your fruit this way. Often bruises don't show up until later, when they turn to soft, mushy spots. Eat bruised fruit first.

What kind of weather is best for harvesting fruits?

Dry, cool weather is best. Avoid picking wet fruits, and if you must pick on hot days, move harvested fruits to a cool place without delay.

Do you have any other advice about harvesting?

Please remember your own safety. Ladders set on moist ground topple easily, so have someone hold the ladder for you as you climb it. Remember that tree limbs laden with fruit may be just short of their breaking point and should not be burdened with your body's weight, too. It's better to let those last few, out-of-reach apples fall to the ground on the next windy day than to risk your limbs for them. Apple-picking tools allow you to pick high-growing fruits from the ground.

THE FRUIT HARVEST

·

Dry, cool weather is best for harvesting fruits; if you must pick on hot days, move harvested fruit to a cool place as soon as possible.

Positive Images, Jerry Howard

INSECT PESTS AND DISEASES OF FRUITS AND BERRIES

•

Ron West

Flathead borers burrow beneath the bark of trees, especially those that are unhealthy or stressed.

Ron West

Finely stippled leaves covered with fine webbing are the calling card of spider mites.

If you take measures to remove all insect pests from your garden, you will remove all of the pests' natural enemies as well. Although the chances are that the pests will one day return, their predators may not. It is best, therefore, to maintain a balance you can live with. Paying attention to the soil, water, fertilizer, and pruning needs of your trees and berries, taking adequate garden sanitation measures, and choosing varieties that are suited to your area's growing conditions will go a long way toward avoiding most problems. In addition, learn to recognize whatever is bothering your trees and plants, so that you can choose an effective course of action in defense, and to take into account local conditions, so that you can anticipate the pests and diseases your plants are most likely to encounter and take preventive measures against them before any damage occurs.

Can you tell me which chemicals should be applied to stop the various pest and disease outbreaks?

Your county Extension Service agent can tell you precisely what works best in your area, and your local nursery, garden center, or hardware store will offer a large selection of pesticides and disease-fighting substances under many different brand names. A number of new natural pesticides on the market are less harmful to people, pets, beneficial animals, and the environment than some chemical pesticides, but even natural pesticides must be used with care (see also pages 88-91).

What is dormant oil?

Applied when the buds have begun to swell, but before any leaf or flower tissue has emerged, dormant oil is a refined petroleum product especially marketed for use on plants. Most dormant oils are sold as spray oils, listed as ''60'' or ''70 sec.'' The numbers refer to a viscosity rating. The lower the number, the less viscous (the thinner) the oil.

Protecting Your Fruit from Animals

ANIMAL PEST	DETERRENT
Gophers	Traps
Deer	Surround young trees with a circle of woven wire. Erect double fences, each 4 feet high, placed 5 feet apart, or a 5-foot-high fence with an angled-out section on top.
Rabbits and rodents	Encircle the base of trunks with hardware cloth. Keep mulches from pressing against the tree.
Birds	Drape trees with bird netting.

•

Insect Pests of Fruits and Their Controls

INSECT PEST	CONTROL
Aphids	Spray with dormant oil to kill eggs during winter. (See also page 86.)
Apple maggots	Promptly gather and destroy infested fruit. Hang commercially available red spheres coated with sticky lure as traps. Spray with wettable rotenone (5-percent) at petal fall and then every two weeks through October.
Black cherry aphids	Spray with dormant oil in early spring. Spray aphids with a strong jet of water combined with 2 or 3 tablespoons of soap per gallon.
Cane borers	Prune off and burn infested portion.
Cherry slugs (pear slugs)	Same control as for black cherry aphid. Hand-pick. Dust with wood ashes, then rinse three days later. Spray with dormant oil or rotenone.
Codling moths	To destroy eggs, spray with dormant oil before buds open. Destroy fruit that falls from trees. Thin infested fruit at ping-pong-ball size. Scrape loose bark from trunk. Remove large weeds and debris from below tree. Hang codling moth pheromone traps: two per large tree, one per small tree. Spray just-hatched larvae with *Bacillus thuringiensis* (Bt). Release trichogramma wasps, beneficial insects that are their natural predators. Plant flowering cover crops such as clover, mustard, sweet alyssum, buckwheat, or daisies.
Flathead borers	Protect trunks and bark from damage by coating trunks of young trees with thinned, white latex paint. Dig out borers from trunk and seal scar with tree-patching compound. Destroy infested wood.
Japanese beetles	Hand-pick. Milky spore disease. Pheromone traps.
Leaf rollers and tiers	Hand-pick.
Mites	Spray with dormant oil when buds are just opening (in summer for pears).
Peach tree borers	Dig cautiously into bark and destroy the larva. Spread mothballs around the trunk and cover them with 3 to 4 inches of soil to kill borers in the trunk. (Remove mothballs before irrigation or winter rains begin, and don't apply in summer.)
Peach twig borers	Dormant oil spray.
Pear psyllas	Dormant oil spray. Summer infestations can be controlled with 2 to 3 sprays applied one week apart.
Pear sawfly	Spray for codling moth in the spring to control sawfly as well.
Plum curculios	Gather fallen fruit daily. Promptly gather and destroy infested fruit. Lay a tarp under the tree and shake the tree branches; collect and destroy fallen curculios. Keep trees well pruned. Apply Imidan (considered by some to be less harmful to people and the environment than rotenone and other botanical pesticides) according to label instructions as soon as insects appear, and again one week later.
Rose chafers	Hand-pick. Place a jar of decomposing rose chafers under the vine.
Scales	Dormant oil spray.
Shothole borers	Prevent sunburn on young trees by coating trunks with thinned, white latex paint. Avoid damage to bark.
Tent caterpillars	Use *Bacillus thuringiensis*.

apple maggot

codling moth

leaf tier

rose chafer

Japanese beetle   peach tree borer   plum curculio   shothole borer   scale

Diseases of Fruits and Their Controls

DISEASE	CONTROL
Apple and pear scab	Remove and burn fallen leaves. Spray with micronized sulphur when buds begin to swell in spring, at petal fall, and twelve days after petal fall. Spray sulphur every week during warm, wet, or damp weather.
Bacterial leaf spot	Remove and burn infected and fallen leaves. Prune for good ventilation. Avoid overfertilization.
Bitter rot (apples)	Remove infected fruit and fruit mummies. Scrape off loose bark. Prune away dead and damaged limbs.
Black knot (plums and prunes)	Plant new trees away from infected trees. Prune away infected growth 4 inches below the infection.
Black and white rot	Prune out diseased branches. Remove fruit mummies. Prune for good ventilation.
Brown rot (stone fruit)	Pick all fruits from trees at harvest. Remove infected fruit, fruit mummies, dead and diseased wood, fallen leaves and fruits. Apply dormant spray. Spray blossoms with bordeaux mixture, fixed copper, or sulphur.
Cedar apple rust	Don't plant near juniper or red cedar (or at least remove galls from nearby junipers).
Crown gall	Avoid injuring trees at planting time and while cultivating. Plant disease-free trees in uninfected soil. Remove galls with disinfected knife and cover wound with tree-patching compound. Remove and burn heavily infected trees.
Crown rot	Supply good soil drainage, and keep trunk dry while watering.
Eutypa dieback (*Cytosporina* canker)	Rough, dark cankers appear on pruning wounds, from which gum may ooze. Sterilize your pruning shears between cuts (use 10-percent bleach and 90-percent water), and paint pruning wounds with pruning compound. Keep the area around the tree clean of dead branches and rotted fruit.
Fireblight	Cut back infected growth 12 inches below diseased portion, sterilizing cutting tool between each cut (use 10-percent bleach and 90-percent water). Apply bordeaux mixture (4 tablespoons per gallon of water) three times weekly during bloom. Control sucking insects, which spread the disease. Prune trees yearly. Avoid overfertilization with nitrogen. Use a sod mulch rather than a cover crop.
Gummosis (or bacterial canker)	Prune for strong branch structure. Avoid injury to bark. Inspect tree for borers and control them (see page 19). Remove badly injured wood.
Peach leaf curl	Spray thoroughly with bordeaux mixture or lime sulphur when leaves drop in fall, and again in spring when the buds have begun to swell, but before they color. Reapply if rain washes away application within 24 hours. Remove and destroy infected leaves.
Powdery mildew (apples)	Prune for good ventilation. Remove mildewed twigs. Spray with sulphur before bloom and biweekly thereafter through spring, especially when days are warm and nights damp.

Photos by Ron West

Bacterial leaf spot.

Peach leaf curl.

Powdery mildew.

How long does it take a fruit tree to bear after it's been planted?

That depends upon the fruit and its variety, whether it is a dwarf or a standard, local climate conditions, and cultivation factors. Some apples and pears require several years to reach bearing age, although many dwarf apple trees bloom after two or three years. Peaches usually bear at three years, as do sour cherry trees. Sweet cherries begin at five to seven years, and plums at six to seven years. Highly vigorous trees are slower to come into bearing than trees that grow at a normal pace. Trees low in vigor because of poor drainage, lack of nitrogen, and injury to the leaves from insect or disease can be slow to begin fruiting.

What are the reasons that fruit trees may fail to bear?

Low winter temperatures, or spring frosts when the trees—especially early-blooming trees such as apricots, peaches, and sweet cherries—are in bloom, may kill the flowers. If prolonged cold, wet weather occurs during fruit bloom, bees will not fly and cross-pollinate. If only one self-sterile tree is planted, flowers will fail to set fruit. Over-fertilization can induce a tree to grow a lot of foliage at the expense of fruit bearing. Trees in shady locations won't set fruit, or will bear only lightly.

Our apple tree produces a lot of fruit, but the fruit is always very small. Is there something wrong with the tree?

No. It is simply setting more fruit than it can grow to maturity. When the fruit is about the size of a ping pong ball, thin it, leaving one apple every 6 to 8 inches. Other types of fruit can be thinned in this way, leaving enough space between fruits to accommodate their size.

Our apple tree sets a lot of fruit, but then much of it falls off while it's still green. What's the matter with it?

The tree is simply thinning its own fruit. As long as enough remains, consider the job well done.

WHY FRUIT TREES FAIL TO BEAR

•

3 *The Fruits We Grow*

Apples; Crabapples *(Malus pumila)*

How large do apple trees grow?

Apple trees come in the widest variety of sizes of any fruit tree, ranging from dwarfs that grow to only 4 feet, to standards that can reach 30 feet. Standard crabapples, smaller than apples, usually grow to about 15 feet. Semidwarf apples are usually about 13 feet.

Should I plant more than one apple tree for adequate pollination?

Most apple varieties are self-fruitful, but they will bear more heavily and dependably if another variety that blooms at about the same time is planted close by. Check with your nursery to make sure that trees you use for pollinators are reliable for that purpose. Mutsu, Gravenstein, Jonagold, Winesap, and certain other varieties, for example, will not pollinate other varieties.

Aren't there a lot of potential pest and disease problems for apple trees?

The codling moth is a significant pest, as is plum curculio. Apple maggot, fireblight, and San Jose scale can also be problems. Apple trees need to be sprayed with dormant oil, insecticides, and disease-controlling substances at the correct times, according to local conditions. See pages 18-20.

◀ *Harvest apples for storage when they are a bit underripe.*

Selected Apple Varieties

NAME	FRUIT DESCRIPTION	USES	TREE CHARACTERISTICS
Akane	Bright red, small fruit with crisp, juicy, white flesh	Cider, drying, eating	Early-bearing; scab- and mildew-resistant
Cortland	Large, round fruit; skin red with blue blush; pure white, crunchy, sweet flesh that resists discoloration after slicing	Cider, cooking, eating, storing	Mid- to late-season; Zones 4-8
Dolgo Crab	Bright red, olive-shaped, ½-inch fruits	Canning, jelly	Self-fruitful; very hardy and disease-resistant; abundant white flowers in spring; slender spreading branches; abundant, glossy, reddish green foliage; needs 400 hours of chilling; Zone 2
Empire	Solid red skin; creamy white, crisp, juicy, flavorful flesh	Cider, eating, storing	Self-fruitful; needs thinning; heavy bearer; Zones 4-7
Golden Delicious	Large fruit with yellow skin and crisp, juicy flesh	Cooking, eating	Self-fruitful; early bearing; skin bruises easily; Zones 5-9
Granny Smith	Large, green fruits; crisp, tart, very juicy, white flesh	Cooking, eating, storing	Needs 500-600 hours of chilling; vigorous; early bearing; heavy producing; needs long growth season (170-190 days from bloom to harvest)
Gravenstein	Highly fragrant; thin skin is light green or orange-yellow with red stripes; yellow-white flesh is crisp and juicy	Cider, cooking, eating	Vigorous; bears in summer; fares best in areas with cool summers; Zones 5-8
Grimes Golden	Yellow, lightly russeted skin; sweet, yellow aromatic flesh	Cider, eating, storing	Moderately resistant to cedar-apple rust and fireblight; Zones 6-8
Jonagold	Large fruits; skin yellow with red strips; crisp, juicy, tart flesh	Cooking, eating, storing	Vigorous; self-sterile; susceptible to mildew and scab; Zones 5-8
Jonathan	Round, red fruits with thin, tough skin; juicy flesh	Cooking, eating, storing	Heavy bearer; disease-resistant; self-fruitful but improves with cross-pollination; needs 700-800 hours of chilling; Zones 5-8
Liberty	Shiny, red fruits with crisp, juicy, yellow flesh	Cooking, eating, storing	Extremely disease-resistant; hardy; vigorous; productive; needs thinning; needs 800 hours of chilling; Zones 4-8
Lodi	Light green to yellow fruits with crisp, juicy flesh	Cooking	Heavy and early bearer; requires pollinator; resists apple scab; Zones 4-8
Macoun	Red skin with a blue blush; firm, juicy, white flesh	Eating	Disease-resistant; popular in the Northeast; needs thinning; tends to bear every other year; resists fireblight; needs 600 hours of chilling; Zones 3-4
McIntosh	Red-striped fruits; white, crisp, aromatic flesh	Cider, cooking, eating, storing	Hardy; heavy bearer; needs thinning; fruits ripen simultaneously; popular in Northeast; resists cedar-apple rust; Zones 4-8 and mild parts of Zone 3
Mutsu (Crispin)	Large, yellow fruits; firm, juicy, spicy flesh	Cider, cooking, eating, storing	Vigorous; heavy and early bearer; self-sterile; resists powdery mildew but susceptible to scab; needs 500-600 hours of chilling; Zones 4-8
Newtown Pippin	Yellow fruits with crisp, aromatic, yellow flesh	Cider, cooking, eating, storing	Large and vigorous; early bearing; self-fruitful; Zones 5-8

Selected Apple Varieties

NAME	FRUIT DESCRIPTION	USES	TREE CHARACTERISTICS
Northern Spy	Skin light green with red stripes; flesh firm, crisp, juicy, and yellow	Cooking, eating, storing	Slow to bear fruit (up to 15 years); heavy bearer; hardy; good in northern states; needs 800 hours of chilling; Zones 4-8
Red Delicious	Dark red, shiny skin; five lobes on the blossom end; tall, tapered shape; crisp, tender, mild, juicy flesh	Eating	Many Delicious varieties; productive and fast growing; self-sterile (needs a pollinator within 100 feet); resists fireblight and cedar-apple rust; Zones 5-8
Rome Beauty (Red)	Large, round, red fruit; white, tart, crunchy flesh	Cider, cooking, eating	Vigorous; early bearing; self-pollinating; Zones 5-8
Spartan	Deep red fruits; aromatic, firm, white flesh	Eating	Early and heavy bearer; self-fruitful (yields increase if planted with Lodi); resists scab, mildew, and fireblight; good in Midwest
Stayman Winesap	Deep red color; tender, juicy, tart, yellow flesh	Cider, cooking, eating	Resists fireblight; needs 600-800 hours of chilling; needs pollinator; Zones 5-8
Winter Banana	Large, pale yellow fruits with a light red to pink blush; crisp, tender, coarse-grained, flavorful flesh	Cider, eating, storing	Bears at a very young age; needs pollinator; needs 100-400 hours of chilling; good in mild-winter West Coast areas; Zones 4-6

A mature standard apple tree is one of the stateliest of trees.

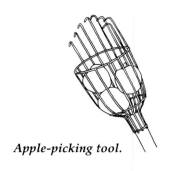

Apple-picking tool.

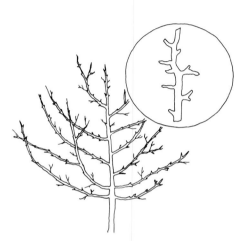

SPUR-TYPE APPLE TREE

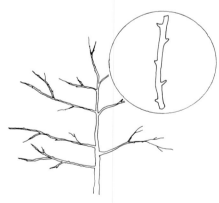

REGULAR APPLE TREE

Spur-type trees have more fruit spurs on each limb and bear from the trunk out.

How are apple trees pruned?

Apples produce fruit on terminal spurs (short, stiff, thin, fruit-bearing branches) on two- to eight-year-old wood. Thin out weak, unproductive, and tangled branches to allow sunlight to penetrate to the center of the tree. Remove old spurs by cutting back the branches they are on. To regulate your tree's height, cut back upper branches to short lateral branches. (See also pages 13-14.)

Should I thin the fruit from my apple tree?

Standard apple trees should be thinned (see page 21), but crabapples need not be.

When should I start harvesting apples?

Harvest apples when the skins change from a dull to a bright color. The seeds of ripe apples are a solid, dark brown. Harvest apples for storage while they're a bit underripe. Don't let ripe fruit hang on the tree.

What are spur-type apple trees?

Spur-type apple trees are extremely productive semidwarfs (12 to 15 feet tall and equally wide), which bear fruiting spurs all along their branches, rather than mostly toward the ends.

I have just moved to Mississippi from New England, where I had several apple trees. Can I grow apple trees in the South?

The only places where apples usually aren't grown is where there are very warm winters (as in southern Florida), extremely dry heat (as in the Nevada desert), or uncommonly fierce weather combined with short growing seasons (as in Montana). Yet there are apple trees even in these places, grown by folks who tend their trees carefully and who have done a little research into unusual and hard-to-find varieties (such as Tropical Beauty and Beverly Hills, both of which are adapted to warm climates, and Honeygold, a very cold-hardy variety).

Apricots *(Prunus armeniaca)*

How can I incorporate apricot trees into my garden design?

Apricots are as ornamental as they are productive, with their soft green, heart-shaped leaves and brilliant white blossoms. Their gnarled trunks and branches lend beauty and interest to a landscape at any time of year. Because the dwarf varieties grow well in containers, gardeners living in climates too cold for apricots can grow dwarfs in tubs set on dollies, and bring them under cover during the winter months.

How big do apricot trees get?

Dwarfs are 8 feet or smaller; semidwarfs, 12 to 15 feet; standards, 15 to 20 feet. All types are usually about as wide as they are tall, depending upon how you prune them.

Can apricot trees be grown outside only in very warm climates?

Apricot trees will grow surprisingly far north, but they won't set fruit, because they have the maddening habit of blossoming so early that subsequent late frosts ruin the fruit. Though it is true that apricot trees will grow in Zones 5 through 9, it is more accurate to say that they will produce fruit where there are *not* heavy, late spring frosts. Even in marginal areas, however, if you choose the proper variety for your locality, and plant an apricot tree in a spot that is neither a frost pocket nor the first place in your yard to receive spring heat (which will cause too-early blossoming), it may bear fruit, if not every year, at least in some years. One of the hardier varieties, such as Moongold, may even thrive in a protected area in Zone 4.

Selected Apricot Varieties

NAME	FRUIT DESCRIPTION	USES	TREE CHARACTERISTICS
Chinese (Mormon Chinese)	Yellow to orange fruits with good flavor	Eating	Late-flowering habit protects it from spring frosts; trees bear at young age; heavy producer; needs 700 hours of chilling
Early Golden	Large, sweet, succulent fruits with smooth, orange-gold skin	Canning, cooking, drying, eating	Self-fruitful, but improved with pollinator; needs 450 hours of chilling; good in South and Southwest; Zones 5-8
Goldcot	Firm, golden yellow skin; tangy, juicy, freestone flesh	Canning, freezing, eating	Late-flowering habit protects it from spring frosts; needs thinning; very hardy; vigorous; heavy-bearing; self-fruitful; good in Northwest; Zones 5-8
Moongold	Soft, golden fruit with firm, sweet, freestone flesh	Canning, eating, preserves	Very hardy (to -25° F.); disease-free; needs Sungold as a pollinator; Zones 4-9
Moorpark	Large, orange fruits with a red blush; juicy, highly aromatic flesh	Canning, drying, eating	Vigorous dwarf; beautiful pinkish white blossoms; good in the Southeast and the West Coast; needs 600 hours of chilling; self-pollinating, but better in pairs; Zones 5-8
Sungold	Gold skin with orange blush; sweet, juicy, freestone flesh	Canning, eating, preserves	Heavy bearer; pink blossoms; pollinate with Moongold; the two are the hardiest of all apricots; Zones 4-9

What is the best place to grow an apricot tree?

Plant apricot trees in well-drained, fertile soil, in a spot that is cool in spring and warm in summer.

Do apricot trees need to be planted in pairs for pollination?

Most varieties are self-fertile, but planting two or more trees assures a maximum harvest, especially in cooler climates.

Do apricot trees need a lot of pruning?

Fruit is borne on one- to four-year-old spurs. Each year, prune heavily to remove old, spent spurs, cutting the old wood right back to the larger branches. If for some reason you cannot prune, make sure to thin the fruit, soon after it sets, to 3- to 4-inch spacings (see page 21).

When should I harvest apricots?

Most varieties ripen all their fruit within a one-week period, and it must be harvested as soon as it begins to soften slightly. Fruit for canning and processing may be picked while it is still slightly hard, but tree-ripened fruit is best for eating fresh or drying. A mature tree can produce as much as 100 pounds of fruit.

How are apricots dried?

Split the apricots open at the seam, remove the pit, and lay the halves open-side-up on a tray. Place them in an oven with a pilot light or dry them outdoors, bringing them under cover at night, until they are shriveled and slightly leathery.

Cherries *(Prunus cerasus; P. avium)*

In what kind of climate must cherry trees be grown?

Although generally cherry trees can be grown in Zones 4 through 9, sweet cherries are more demanding than sour cherries. Depending upon the variety, sweet cherries need at least 800 hours of winter chill and cannot withstand high summer temperatures. Significant rainfall in the weeks before the harvest can make the fruit split. Humid climates are not favorable to sweet cherries, nor is foggy weather. Sour cherries are easier to grow, so if you have hot summers where you live, or humidity, fog, or a short chilling season, start with the sours. Sour cherries make better preserves and pies, and when tree-ripened they can be delicious eaten fresh, with a taste more tart and sweet than sour.

Should I plant more than one cherry tree for cross-pollination?

Sour cherries are self-pollinating. Two, and sometimes three, sweet cherry trees must be planted within pollinating distance of each other.

Do cherry trees require a lot of watering?

The ground beneath cherry trees should be kept moist, because the trees have shallow root systems that can easily dry out. Use organic mulches. Water newly planted trees every week; older, established trees may be watered less often. Sour cherries tolerate drought better than sweets. Water the trees after the harvest, and every three to four weeks thereafter if there are no summer rains.

Selected Cherry Varieties

NAME	FRUIT DESCRIPTION	TREE CHARACTERISTICS	POLLINATOR
Bing (sweet)	Large, firm, aromatic, sweet fruits; dark red skin	Grows best in dry, warm summers; good in the West; does not do well in hot, humid weather; fruit ripens all at once; needs 700 hours of chilling; Zones 5-8	Black Tartarian or Van
Black Tartarian (sweet)	Dark, heart-shaped, soft fruits with sweet, rich flavor	Early-blooming and -ripening tree; heavy bearing; good pollinator; grows 30 feet tall; needs 700 hours of chilling; Zones 5-7	Most other varieties (Lambert not recommended)
Lambert (sweet)	Large, sweet, firm fruit with dark skin and very dark red flesh	Late blooming and bearing; not resistant to splitting; needs 800 hours of chilling; Zones 5-7	Black Tartarian, Rainier, Stella, or Van
Montmorency (sour)	Bright red fruit with firm, yellow flesh	The classic tart cherry; heavy bearing; needs 700 hours of chilling; Zones 5-7	Self-fruitful
Napoleon, or Royal Ann (sweet)	Yellow skin with red blush; sweet, juicy flesh	Ripens midseason; tree grows 20-25 feet tall; heavy bearer; needs 700 hours of chilling; Zones 5-7	Black Tartarian, Stella, or Van
North Star (sour)	Large, light red fruits with red flesh and juice	Naturally dwarf tree, grows 6-12 feet tall; heavy and early bearing; disease-resistant; very hardy; needs 1000 hours of chilling; Zones 4-8	Self-fruitful
Rainier (sweet)	Yellow fruit with a red blush; firm, fine-textured flesh	Early and heavy bearing; split-resistant; very hardy; tolerates hot summers; need 700 hours of chilling	Bing, Black Tartarian, Lambert, Napoleon, Stella, or Van
Stella (sweet)	Heart-shaped, dark red fruit with sweet, juicy flesh	Vigorous and hardy trees; grows 25-30 feet tall; good pollinator; bears early and abundantly; resistant to splitting; needs 700 hours of chilling; Zones 5-8	Self-fruitful
Van (sweet)	Large, dark, firm fruit	Split-resistant fruit; hardy; excellent pollinator; needs 700 hours of chilling; Zones 5-7	Bing, Lambert, Napoleon, Rainier, or Stella

How much pruning and thinning should I give my cherry trees?

Sweet cherries are best trained to a vase shape (see page 13) to allow light to penetrate into the center of the tree and to make picking easier. Prune bare-rooted trees down to 24 to 36 inches when you plant them. You needn't thin the fruit of cherry trees.

How can I tell when it's time to harvest cherries?

Harvest Bing and other dark-skinned cherries when the fruit has turned thoroughly dark. Don't be too anxious to get them off the tree—the longer they stay on, the sweeter they'll be. When you pick, leave the stems on the cherries, and take care not to damage the fruiting spurs that the cherries are attached to. Store cherries in the vegetable crisper of your refrigerator until you are ready to use them. Under storage, they need cool, humid air.

How can I keep birds from harvesting all my cherries before I get to them?

The only sure way is to cover your trees with protective netting. It is much easier to accomplish this on dwarf and semidwarf trees. Some people believe birds are less attracted to yellow or golden cherries, such as Golden Sweet.

Sweet Van cherries are hardy and resistant to splitting.

Stark Brothers Nurseries and Orchards

What insects cause problems for cherry trees?

The principal insect pests include black cherry aphids, eye-spotted bud moths, and pear slugs (cherry slugs). The cherry fruit fly (apple maggot) can be a problem in the Northwest. See pages 18-19 for controls.

Are there any diseases that attack cherry trees?

Bacterial canker is one of the most serious, because it can kill young cherry trees. Also known as gummosis, the disease manifests itself by large gobs of amber-colored gum oozing from the branches. Cherry trees growing in areas of high rainfall may experience brown rot. See page 20 for controls.

Our summers are very hot. What can I do to prevent sunscald?

Paint the trunks with a white latex paint to prevent sunscald (extensive cell damage to the bark, caused by the dark trunk getting hotter than the air).

Figs (*Ficus carica*)

May figs be grown only in warm climates?

Although the fig tree and its soft fruit look tropical, and figs are most commonly grown in areas with a Mediterranean climate, they are actually hardy down to 15° F. and can be grown as container plants almost anywhere, so long as they are moved under cover during winter. The plants grow as shrubs in colder areas. Young trees may be damaged by 25° to 27° F. temperatures, and killed by cold at 22° F. In the West and the South, figs can stay in the ground all year, as they are best suited to Zones 8 through 10. In Zone 7, figs may survive in a warm garden location, especially if the trunk is wrapped with an insulating material such as fiberglass insulation or burlap stuffed with dried leaves or straw during the winter. Cover the insulation with waterproof plastic, tied closed at the top, and mulch the root zone deeply. Unprotected fig bushes that die back to the ground will grow up again when the warm weather resumes. Wherever you plant a fig tree, it must receive full sun.

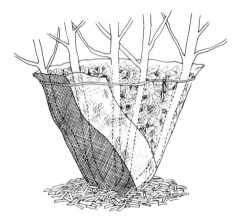

Fig trees may be protected over winter in cool climates by wrapping the trunks with burlap stuffed with dried leaves or straw.

What kind of soil do fig trees need?

Fig trees do best in heavy clay soil that is poor in nutrients, but they must have good drainage. The soil should not be acid, nor should it contain excessive boron, sodium, or herbicides. Too much nitrogen encourages lush foliage at the expense of a heavy fruit crop.

Must I plant more than one fig tree for cross-pollination?

No. Almost all figs are self-fertile.

Is it difficult to espalier fig trees?

Fig trees are quite amenable to training, and make excellent espaliers. They are usually trained with three to five principal branches. The tree can be kept quite low and wide by yearly pruning of the top growth during the dormant season. (See pages 13-14.)

Should I thin the fruit on my fig tree?

Though fig trees often set very heavy crops, their fruit does not need thinning. In the West most figs bear two crops. The first, or *breba*, crop comes in early summer, and the second in fall.

Should I fertilize my fig tree?

Do not fertilize fig trees unless they are growing in extremely poor soil and are putting out less than 1 foot of new growth a year. If so, and you know that the cause is poor soil rather than unsuitable weather, add small amounts of nitrogen—about 1 pound for a mature tree—in winter. The best soil amendment for figs is bulky organic matter, which will provide the water retention and drainage that the trees need.

Will fig trees tolerate drought?

Yes, but for the best crop, water trees deeply whenever the soil dries out 3 to 4 inches below the surface. Stop watering as soon as the fruit begins to swell.

How will I know when it's time to harvest my figs?

In general, figs are ripe and ready to be harvested when they are heavy enough to weigh their stems down. The easiest way to tell is simply to pick a few (with their stems attached) and bite into them to see if they taste ripe.

Selected Fig Varieties

NAME	DESCRIPTION	USES	CHARACTERISTICS
Brown Turkey	Purplish green to mahogany-brown skin; sweet, juicy, strawberry-colored flesh	Canning, drying, eating, jam	Hardiest of all figs; bushy plant grows to 10 feet; self-pollinating; winter hardy; needs 100 hours of chilling; Zone 5 with protection
Celeste	Violet-brown skin; light pink, firm, sweet flesh	Eating	Hardy; self-pollinating; popular in Southeast; Zones 7-10
Conadria	Large fruits with light green skin; whitish pink flesh	Drying, eating	Very productive; good in very hot-summer areas (West Coast); needs 100 hours of chilling
Texas Everbearing	Fruit dark brown with green cast; amber flesh	Preserves	Bears fruit from late summer to late fall; small tree, good for container growing; self-pollinating; good in Southwest; Zones 7-10

How are figs stored?

Don't store them stacked up or they may ferment. If you plan on canning them, harvest figs just before they are ripe. If you plan on drying them, leave them on the tree until they begin to shrivel and drop off; then pick them, arrange them on trays, and dry them in the sun or a slow oven.

Do figs have many pest and disease problems?

Figs are virtually pest- and disease-free, and do not need to be sprayed.

Peaches; Nectarines *(Prunus persica; P. persica var. nuciperica)*

What is the difference between peaches and nectarines?

Only the smooth, fuzzless skin of the nectarine.

In what regions will peach trees survive?

The hardier cultivars will survive temperatures of -10° F. once they're well established. Generally speaking, peaches and nectarines can be grown in Zones 6 through 9. The crucial factors are the depth of winter temperatures and the lateness of spring frosts. Cold, damp spring weather is not suitable to peaches, nor are cool or humid summers. Varieties with low chill requirements (see page 2) will bear in Zones 9 and 10; most varieties need 600 to 900 hours of chilling. The ideal peach-growing climate is found in the inland valleys of California, where spring comes early, and summers are entirely without rain and of low humidity.

I live near Boston. Is there any chance I could grow peaches?

Contact your local Extension Service agent and ask for a list of varieties best suited to your area. There may be a warm location on your property where a peach tree will grow, or you could use a genetic dwarf peach or nectarine in a container, which could be brought under cover during sub-zero weather. These miniature trees are charming and much easier to manage than large, in-ground peach trees. Give peaches and nectarines full sun, and avoid frost pockets.

What kind of soil do peach trees need?

A well-drained, rich, sandy loam is best for peaches. Heavy clay soils should be modified with large amounts of bulky organic material prior to planting. Continue adding more organic matter throughout the lifetime of the tree.

Is it necessary to plant pairs of peach trees for pollination?

Most varieties are self-fertile.

Are there any advantages to growing dwarf peach or nectarine trees?

There are some excellent genetic dwarf varieties (see page 7). If you plant them in tubs, you can move them out of the rain and thus avoid peach leaf curl without spraying. In addition, it takes only a small amount of netting to protect the fruit from birds.

Selected Peach Varieties

NAME	FRUIT DESCRIPTION	USES	TREE CHARACTERISTICS
Belle of Georgia	Soft, aromatic fruit with white flesh; freestone flesh tinged with red	Canning, desserts, eating	Hardy; vigorous; self-fruitful; disease-resistant; needs 800-850 hours of chilling; Zones 5-8
Bonanza	Yellow flesh with red blush; freestone	Eating	Genetic dwarf, grows 4-5 feet tall; masses of large, pink, self-fruitful blossoms; very productive; needs 250-500 hours of chilling; good for South and West
Early Elberta	Large, yellow-fleshed, freestone fruits with sweet, rich flavor	Canning, eating, freezing	Hardy, productive, and reliable; self-fruitful; best for warm climates; needs 500 hours of chilling; Zones 5-8
Elberta	Skin yellow with a pink blush; juicy, yellow, freestone flesh; peels easily	Canning, eating, freezing, jam	Disease-resistant; productive, though tends to drop mature fruits; self-fruitful; needs 800-950 hours of chilling; Zones 5-8
Hale Haven	Large, oval-shaped, yellow fruit with red blush, tough skin; firm, sweet, juicy flesh	Canning, freezing	Abundant producer; vigorous; hardy; needs 850 hours of chilling; Zones 5-8
Honey Babe	Yellow skin with deep red blush; sweet, freestone, red-speckled, orange fruit	Eating	Genetic dwarf, grows 3-5 feet tall; good in West; dense foliage; self-fertile; needs 500-600 hours of chilling; Zones 6-9
Indian Blood Cling	Crimson red skin and flesh; clingstone; tart flavor	Baking, eating, preserves	Resistant to bacterial leaf spot and brown rot; dependable; heavy bearing; needs 750-900 hours of chilling
J.H. Hale	Large, round, uniform, firm fruits with yellow flesh; skin deep crimson and almost fuzzless	Canning, eating	Must have a pollinator; excellent keeper; needs 850-900 hours of chilling; Zones 5-8
Red Haven	Red, nearly fuzzless fruit; firm, yellow, freestone flesh	Canning, eating, freezing	Hardy; self-fruitful; tolerant of cold and leaf spot; heavy yielding and reliable; needs thinning; good in lower Midwest; needs 800-950 hours of chilling; Zones 5-8
Redskin	Large fruit with yellow, freestone, non-browning flesh beneath a red skin	Canning, eating, freezing	Vigorous and productive; resistant to bacterial spot; needs 750 hours of chilling; Zones 5-8
Reliance	Medium-sized fruit with yellow skin, blushed red; bright yellow, juicy, sweet flesh; freestone	Canning, freezing	Self-fruitful; best choice for cold winter areas (to -25° F.); needs 1,000 hours of chilling; Zones 5-8
Rio Oso Gem	Large, yellow fruit with red blush; firm, freestone flesh; excellent flavor	Eating, freezing	Short-lived, not vigorous; self-fertile; needs 800-850 hours of chilling

Selected Nectarine Varieties

NAME	FRUIT DESCRIPTION	TREE CHARACTERISTICS
Fantasia	Skin yellow with red blush; smooth, firm, freestone flesh	Heavy bearing; self-fruitful; susceptible to bacterial leaf spot; needs 500-600 hours of chilling
Flavortop	Large, red-over-yellow fruits; juicy, sweet, fine-textured, freestone flesh	Self-fruitful; vigorous; heavy-bearing; large, showy blossoms; good in both East and West; needs 650 hours of chilling
Garden Beauty	Yellow, clingstone flesh; usually sweet	Genetic dwarf, grows 4-5½ feet tall; large, double, dark pink blossoms; self-fruitful; needs 500-600 hours of chilling
Mericrest	Smooth, dark red fruit with sweet, juicy, yellow, freestone flesh and tangy flavor	Self-fruitful; resists brown rot and bacterial leaf spot; needs 800 hours of chilling; hardiest nectarine; Zones 5-8
Nectar Babe	Large red fruits with sweet, yellow, freestone flesh	Genetic dwarf, growing no more than 6 feet tall; quite productive; needs pollinator (Honey Babe); needs 500-600 hours of chilling; Zone 9
Red Gold	Skin mostly red, with some yellow; deep golden, firm, juicy, freestone flesh; outstanding flavor	Winter hardy; extremely productive and vigorous; self-fruitful; susceptible to bacterial spot and mildew; needs 850 hours of chilling; Zones 5-8

Will I have to give my peach trees much pruning?

Heavy annual pruning is necessary for good crops, because peaches and nectarines bear fruit only on *new* wood. Train young trees to a vase shape (see page 13), keeping in mind that good light penetration is vital. When the trees are mature, begin removing one half of the new wood late in the dormant season. Prune the tops of peach and nectarine trees annually to maintain a workable height.

Check with your local Extension Service to determine the best method of pruning for your area. Each climate dictates certain pruning programs that may not apply to other climates.

Should I fertilize my peach trees?

Advice for fertilizing varies from one area to another, so it is best to contact your local Extension Service agent on this matter. Here are a few rules of thumb. Peaches and nectarines are heavy feeders, and should be fertilized at least once a year, preferably in late spring just as the new growth gets going. Fertilizing a peach or nectarine after the harvest can be risky business, because ensuing cold weather could damage the new, lush growth that results from fertilization and thus weaken the tree. During the growing season, mulch with compost or manure around mature trees to add some nitrogen and other plant nutrients and increase the content of organic matter in the soil.

Is it true that peaches and nectarines are prone to many pests and diseases?

Leaf curl and brown rot are the foremost diseases. Powdery mildew must be contended with in humid climates. Peach tree

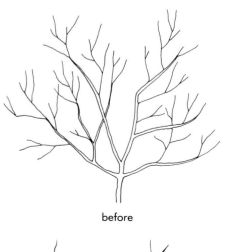

before

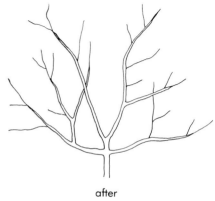

after

Peach trees should be heavily pruned to a vase shape.

Before peaches are the size of ping pong balls, thin fruits, leaving about 6 inches between each one.

borer is the major insect pest, though plum curculio, San Jose scale, and aphids can also be problems. See pages 18-20 for controls, and contact your local Extension Service for the spraying program that has been developed specifically for your area.

Should I thin peach fruit?

Thin the fruit before it reaches ping-pong-ball size, leaving 6 to 8 inches between fruits of early ripening varieties, and 4 to 6 inches between late ripeners. Leaving too many fruits on the branches weakens the tree considerably.

When can I harvest my peaches?

A ripe peach or nectarine should come free with just a gentle tug. Keep fresh-picked fruit in a cool place, and eat it as soon as possible.

Pears *(Pyrus communis; P. pyrifolia)*

What is the difference between European and Asian varieties of pears?

The most common European varieties of pears grown in North America include Bartlett, Bosc, Anjou, Seckel, and Comice. They range in color from brown, green, and red to many shades of yellow, and in form from almost oval to bell-shaped. Asian pears, on the other hand, look much like apples, with very juicy and crisp, mild-flavored, somewhat coarse-textured flesh. They are grown much like European pears, though they are slightly hardier; they need cross-pollination from European or other Asian pears.

What kind of climate do pears need?

Depending on the variety, pears may be grown in Zones 3 through 9. All pears need a certain amount of winter chill, which makes them difficult to grow in frost-free areas, and yet any pear will suffer blossom damage from spring frosts. Give all pear trees a sunny, low-frost location.

Are pear trees particular about the soil they grow in?

Pear trees prefer deep, somewhat heavy soils containing good amounts of organic matter. They tolerate wet soils better than do apples and peaches.

Should I plant more than one pear tree for cross-pollination?

Yes, they should be planted in pairs or larger groupings. Although some varieties are self-fertile, they will produce better crops if another variety of a similar bloom period is growing nearby.

Selected Pear Varieties

NAME	FRUIT DESCRIPTION	USES	TREE CHARACTERISTICS
Anjou (Beurre D'Anjou)	Large, light green fruit; mild, aromatic, somewhat dry flesh	Canning, drying, eating, storing	European; large; vigorous; hardy; needs pollinator (Bosc or Bartlett); somewhat blight-resistant; needs 800 hours of chilling
Bartlett	Large, golden fruit blushed with red; sweet, juicy, white flesh	Canning, eating, preserves	European; vigorous; highly productive; long-lived; partially self-fruitful in arid or warm climates, but needs pollinator elsewhere (Anjou or Bosc); needs 800 hours of chilling; Zones 5-7
Bosc (Beurre Bosc)	Long, thin-necked, tapered fruits; heavily russeted skin; firm, rich, sweet, aromatic flesh	Baking, drying, eating	European; slow-growing but productive; needs pollinator; susceptible to fireblight in warm, moist areas; needs 800-900 hours of chilling; Zones 5-8
Chojuro (Old World)	Skin thick, brown, russetted; flesh firm, highly flavored	Storing	Asian; needs thinning; needs pollinator (Shinseiki, Hosui, Bartlett); needs 450-500 hours of chilling
Clapp's Favorite	Large, elongated, lemon-yellow fruit with russet flecks; fine-grained, sweet, white flesh	Canning, eating	European; strong, hardy, vigorous tree; susceptible to fireblight
Comice	Very large, thick-skinned, yellow fruits with red blush; juicy, firm, sweet flesh	Eating	European; very late ripening; large; somewhat fireblight-resistant; does well in Oregon and California; needs 600 hours of chilling
Hosui	Brownish orange skin; juicy, sweet flesh similar to a melon	Storing	Asian; needs pollinator (Chojuro, Bartlett, Shinseiki); popular in California and the Northwest; needs 450-500 hours of chilling
Kieffer	Large, yellow fruits with red blush; crisp, juicy white flesh	Baking, canning, preserves, storing	European; hardy; vigorous; dependable; tolerates hot weather, but grows well in most areas; highly resistant to fireblight; needs 350 hours of chilling; Zones 4-9
Moonglow	Large fruit is dull yellow with red blush; soft, white flesh	Canning, eating, storing	European; developed by USDA for blight resistance; bears heavily while still young; needs pollinator; excellent pollinator for other varieties; needs 700 hours of chilling; Zones 5-8
Seckel (Sugar Pear)	Small, yellow-green skin with red blush; extremely sweet, very juicy flesh	Canning, eating, pickling and spicing	European; bears abundantly; some blight resistance; self-fruitful but better with cross-pollination; grows only 15-20 feet tall; needs 500-800 hours of chilling; Zones 5-8
Shinseiki	Large, round, yellow fruit; mild, sweet, crisp, creamy white flesh	Eating, storing	Asian; heavy-bearing; needs pollinator (Bartlett, Chojuro, Hosui); moderate resistance to fireblight; needs 450 hours of chilling; Zones 6-9
20th Century (Nijiseiki)	Medium-sized, yellow fruit with green mottle; quite juicy, mild, crisp flesh	Eating, storing	Asian; ornamental tree with large, glossy leaves; productive; tolerates drought and heat, but not disease resistant; needs 450-500 hours of chilling; Zones 6-9

Do pear trees need much pruning?

Pears have an upright growth habit that is conducive to training for a vase shape (see page 13), but like apples, they produce on long-lived spurs and need little pruning. Remove tangled, weak, and diseased limbs, and cut away wood that does not conform to the shape you desire for the tree. Young trees can be trained to three or four scaffold branches emanating from the trunk.

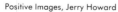

Positive Images, Jerry Howard

Should I thin pear fruit after it sets?

Both European and Asian varieties should be thinned to stand 4 to 6 inches apart if the tree sets a heavy crop. Often they don't need thinning at all.

How much fertilizing do pear trees need?

Excess nitrogen encourages lush stem growth that is highly susceptible to fireblight. Do not fertilize a pear tree that is putting out at least 12 inches of new growth a year and setting a good amount of fruit. If you do fertilize, do so sparingly. A thick mulch of organic matter is highly beneficial, and will usually provide an adequate supply of nutrients.

When should I harvest my pears?

Asian varieties should be left on the tree to ripen. After you pick them they will keep in the refrigerator for months. European pears must be picked at full size but while still green and quite unripe. The seeds of a harvest-ready pear will be light brown to brown. To ripen the harvested fruit, keep it in a cool (50°-70° F.), dark place until the blossom end turns slightly soft. Placing several pears together in a paper bag hastens the process. Check the fruits often for ripeness. Winter varieties, such as Anjou and Bosc, should be held at cool (32° to 34° F.) temperatures from one to four months. Take these pears out of the refrigerator a week before you plan to eat them.

Both Asian and European pears should be picked when they are still unripe; the seeds of a harvest-ready pear are light brown to brown.

What can I do to combat pear fireblight?

Fireblight is the great enemy of pears, so much so that in some areas pears are impossible to grow because the disease is so widespread. Ask your local Extension Service agent if you aren't sure about your area. Plant resistant varieties, and check your trees closely in the spring for any shriveled, darkened growth (a burned appearance). Cut it off immediately, taking with it 9 inches of undiseased wood as well. After each cut, sterilize your cutting shears (use 10-percent bleach and 90-percent water). Bordeaux mixture applied at a solution of 1 tablespoon per quart of water when 20 percent of the blossoms have opened, and again when 70 percent of them have opened, and once more at full blossom, will help control the problem. (See also page 20.)

Aphids and other sucking insects spread the disease, so control them as described on pages 19 and 86.

Are there other pests or diseases that afflict pears?

Pear psylla, pear slug, codling moth, and most other insects that bother apples. For controls, see page 19.

Persimmons *(Diospyros virginiana* and *D. Kaki)*

Are persimmons hard to grow?

Perhaps there is no fruit tree so beautiful and easy to care for as the persimmon. It needs no spraying or pruning (except perhaps for shaping or removing dead or tangled limbs), little or no fertilizing, and, once established, no irrigation in most regions. It can withstand damper soil than most trees.

What do persimmon trees look like?

They are medium to large sized and well shaped, with large, pointed, oval leaves, and serve as excellent shade givers. The foliage, which turns yellow, orange, and red in autumn, drops from the trees to leave a colorful display of ripened fruit hanging on the branches until winter.

What do persimmons taste like?

The fruits are delicious, whether eaten fresh, sliced in sweet salads, baked in persimmon puddings, breads, and cookies, made into wine, or dried—they taste something like dates and are a great delicacy in Asia.

What is the difference between American and Oriental persimmons?

The American variety (*Diospyros virginiana*), grows in the wild from Connecticut south, and west from Kansas to Texas. It is hardy to -25° F. Its fruits are small (from 1 to 2 inches in diameter), with seeds that Native Americans used for making bread. Notably, the fruit must be fully ripe before it can be eaten; it is otherwise unbearably astringent. Oriental persimmons (*Diospyros Kaki*) are larger and often seedless. The trees are less hardy than the trees of the American species, but will withstand winter temperatures down to 0° F. once established. The non-astringent types may be eaten while still firm, while the astringent varieties, such as Hachiya, must be fully ripe to be eaten fresh.

How large do persimmon trees grow?

American persimmons grow to 40 feet; Oriental types, to 30 feet. You can easily prune either type down to smaller sizes, including espaliered configurations, although you need only remove damaged, dead, or crossed limbs. Fruit thinning is unnecessary.

Where will persimmons grow?

American persimmons will grow in Zones 4 through 8; Oriental persimmons, in Zones 7 through 10.

Are persimmons fussy about their soil needs?

Though persimmons prefer a loamy, well-drained soil, they tolerate wet soils fairly well. Plant in a sunny location so the fruit will ripen.

Do persimmons need to be planted in groups?

With the exception of Meader, American persimmons need a pollinator nearby. Oriental persimmons produce seedless fruit without a pollinator.

When are persimmons harvested?

American persimmons ripen in the fall, about a month earlier than Oriental types. Harvest them before the first frost, when the fruit has colored but is still firm. If you pick them before they are fully ripe, set them stem-end-down at room temperature until soft. Nonastringent oriental types can be eaten right away; place astringent types stem down at room temperature until they are very soft and sweet.

Selected Persimmon Varieties

NAME	FRUIT DESCRIPTION	USES	TREE CHARACTERISTICS
Early Golden	Large, sweet fruits; good flavor	Canning, eating	American; somewhat self-pollinating, but better with a pollinator; hardy
Fuyu	Round and flat-shaped, shiny, orange-red fruit; nonastringent; delicious, mild, sweet flesh	Drying, eating (peeled), freezing	Oriental; self-fruitful; hardy; needs 200 hours of chilling
Hachiya	Large, acorn-shaped fruits; deep orange skins; very sweet when soft and ripe; astringent	Cooking, drying	Oriental; extremely ornamental tree, especially with bright fall foliage; self-fruitful; needs 200 hours of chilling; Zones 7-9
Meader	Orange skin with red blush; sweet, high-quality fruit	Canning, eating	American; hardy; productive; self-fruitful, very ornamental tree with large, dark green foliage; bears early; good in colder areas (to -35° F.); ripens in October
Tanenashi	Astringent until fully ripe; seedless; large orange-red fruits with excellent flavor	Eating	Oriental; grows to 40 feet; self-pollinating; heavy bearing

Plums and Prunes (*Prunus* spp.)

Are plums difficult to grow?

Plums are one of the easiest fruits to grow. They come in the widest variety of colors, shapes, flavors, and sizes of all fruits. There is at least one plum variety that will grow in any of Zones 3 through 10. You haven't tasted a good plum until you've had one sun-ripened on the tree!

What is the difference between a plum and a prune?

Prunes are made from plums that, because they are small and not too juicy, dry easily. Prunes are usually made from the European-type plums.

What are the differences between European, Japanese, and American plums?

The fruit of European plums is usually small and egg-shaped, with dry, very sweet flesh (although some varieties are juicy and unsuitable for drying); the trees are upright and need little

Underwood plums, a Japanese-American cross with yellow flesh and a mild flavor.

Stark Brothers Nurseries and Orchards

thinning or pruning. European plum trees are hardier (Zones 5-8), later blooming, and later ripening than Japanese types.

The large, soft, juicy fruits of the Japanese plums are usually born on branches that tend to hang, or "weep." Their flesh ranges from sweet to tart, some types having sweet outer flesh and tart flesh close to the pit. The trees are less hardy than European types (Zones 5-9). They blossom very early in spring, and their foliage is lighter green than that of European plums.

American plum trees, usually called bush or cherry plums, are by far the hardiest of the three types (Zones 3-7). Native American plums are tart and tough-skinned, good for jellies and sauces. American hybrid plums will thrive where weather conditions are too harsh for other fruits. You can also choose from hybrid crosses of American and Japanese plums, or the native bush or tree forms. Check with your local Extension Service for the best varieties for your area.

Selected Plum Varieties

NAME	FRUIT DESCRIPTION	USES	TREE CHARACTERISTICS
Burbank	Large, purple fruits with firm, juicy flesh; semifreestone; excellent, sweet flavor	Canning, eating	Japanese; naturally small tree (12-15 feet); needs 400 hours of chilling; Zones 5-9
Green Gage	Yellow-green skin; sweet, amber flesh	Canning, cooking, eating, preserving	European; hardy; productive; self-fruitful; needs 500 hours of chilling
Methley	Skin purple with red blush; red, sweet, juicy flesh; distinctive, good flavor	Eating, jelly	Japanese; bears abundantly and consistently; self-fertile; needs 150-250 hours of chilling; Zones 5-9
Ozark Premier	Very large fruits; red skin; yellow, firm, juicy, clingstone flesh; sweet, tangy flavor		Japanese; good in South and Midwest; best with pollinator (other Japanese); Zones 5-9
Santa Rosa	Large, purple-red fruit; purple flesh	Canning, eating	Japanese; vigorous; productive; self-fruitful, but better near other Japanese varieties; very popular in the West; needs 300 hours of chilling; Zones 5-9
Shiro	Large, yellow fruits; yellow, clingstone flesh; sweet, well-flavored, extra juicy	Canning, cooking, eating, preserving	Japanese; reliable; prolific; needs pollinator (Methley, Ozark Premier); needs 150-500 hours of chilling; Zones 5-9
Stanley Prune	Large, dark blue fruits with yellow-green, freestone flesh; highly sweet	Canning, cooking, drying, eating, preserving	European; heavy- and early-bearing; self-pollinating, but better planted with other variety; good for North and Midwest; needs 900 hours of chilling; Zones 5-8
Underwood	Dark red skin; yellow flesh; mild flavor		Japanese-American cross; needs pollinator; recommended for North (hardy to -50° F.), but grows in Zone 8 as well

How big do plum trees get?

Depending on the rootstock on which they are grown, plum trees usually range from 10 to 15 feet in height. European types can be espaliered; bush types can be grown as hedges.

Where should I plant plum trees?

Give plums full sun and well-drained soil. European plums prefer heavy soils, while the Japanese varieties prefer light, loamy soils.

Do plums need pollinator trees nearby?

American plums are self-fertile; European plums, too, are self-fertile, but produce more heavily with a nearby pollinator; Japanese plums must have a pollinator either nearby or grafted onto the same tree.

Do plum trees require a lot of pruning?

American varieties grown as bushes should have their shoots thinned out every two or three years. European plums don't need much pruning other than the removal of unwanted, dead, or tangled limbs, although young trees should be trained to a modified leader or vase shape. Japanese plums need heavy pruning to remove rampant, bushy growth; they are best trained to a vase shape. The fruit of all varieties is borne on both new and old wood; fruit should be thinned to 4- to 5-inch spacings.

How much fertilizer should I give my plum trees?

Plums are smallish trees that bear extremely heavy crops. A thick organic mulch will add nitrogen to the soil. This may be all the tree needs, but many gardeners provide yearly applications of compost and manure.

Can plum trees survive drought?

Yes, once established. Trees growing in areas with dry summers need to be watered deeply whenever the soil dries out 3 to 4 inches beneath the surface.

How ripe should plums be for harvesting if I plan to cook them?

Fruits intended for cooking should be harvested while slightly underripe. Store the fruit in the refrigerator or other cool place, and cook it soon. Plums that will be dried to make prunes should be gathered from the ground promptly after they've fallen from the tree.

Ron West

Plum trees should be grown in full sun, in well-drained soil.

BERRIES AND GRAPES

Maggie Oster

A plastic snake draped in a blueberry bush will frighten away birds that compete for the harvest.

Blueberries *(Vaccinium* spp.)

What are the climate needs of blueberries?

Highbush blueberries can be grown in most areas of the United States, but they are best suited to regions that don't often get temperatures below -20° F. and where there are at least 800 hours of chilling (see page 2).

What kind of soil do blueberries require?

Fertile, acid soil (pH of 4.5 to 5), with a lot of organic material and good drainage.

What guidelines can you suggest for helping me determine how many blueberry bushes I should plant?

A healthy, six- to eight-year-old plant can produce up to 10 quarts of fruit per bush. Each mature plant takes up about 4 to 5 feet; the bushes should be planted about 6 feet apart in rows, with about 8 to 10 feet between rows.

How should I plant blueberry bushes?

If possible, plant on a cloudy afternoon as soon as the ground can be worked in the spring. Although blueberries can be planted in the fall, spring planting is safer and is recommended in most areas. Prune off any damaged or excessively long roots, any weak or broken wood, and all flower buds. Plant bushes 1 to 2 inches deeper than the plants grew in the nursery.

Do blueberries need to be planted in pairs for pollination?

Although they are generally self-fruitful, interplanting cultivars will improve yields.

What kind of care must I give blueberries?

Fertilize them two or three times a year, prune once a year, and make sure they have enough water—they need a constant moisture supply for best growth. Use soaker hoses to avoid getting ripening berries wet or they may split. Apply about an inch of water during each watering.

How should I fertilize blueberries?

The first application should be made about one month after planting. Apply about ½ cup of 5-10-10 or 10-10-10 fertilizer per bush in a broad band at least 6 inches, but not more than 12 inches, from the base. Repeat in early July, and, if plants are not vigorous, again in fall after the leaves drop. Mature plants will need about twice this amount of fertilizer each year, two-thirds at the beginning of bloom and the remainder about five or six months later. Do not apply fertilizer too early in the autumn or you may encourage late growth that can winterkill. Because blueberries prefer acid soil, do not use bonemeal or wood ashes around your plants.

What other care do blueberries need?

Cultivate them frequently, but shallowly, and mulch with an organic material to a depth of about 6 inches. Prune to remove diseased or broken wood and to encourage new wood for future seasons' fruits (see illustration).

What are some good blueberry varieties?

Try Flordablue in the South. A good early variety is Collins; midseason, Patriot, Bluecrop, Berkeley, and Blueray; late season, Elliott's Blueberry and Herbert. Be sure to choose a variety suited to your geographic area.

Grapes (*Vitus* spp.)

Are grapes restricted to certain geographic areas?

With literally thousands of different grape varieties suited to a wide range of climates and soils, there is some variety of grape that will flourish in all parts of the United States and in several Canadian provinces. The best grape climates are regions where the growing season is 150 to 180 days, where relative humidity is low, and where summer rains are sparse rather than frequent. Choose the most suitable varieties for your area and plant them in the most sunny, sheltered, well-drained place you can find on your property.

Do I have to provide support for my grape vines?

Although grapes can be grown ornamentally along fences, for best harvest results train vines to grow on a trellis system (see illustration). Be sure to set end posts securely, 3 feet deep and

before pruning

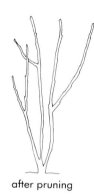

after pruning

Thin young blueberry bushes (2 to 5 years old) by removing all dead and diseased wood, and about one-fourth of their main branches.

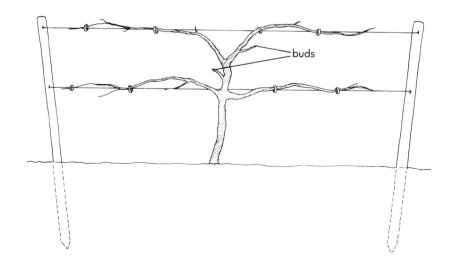

buds

To prune grapevines, during the dormant period following the second or third growing season, choose four of the strongest canes for arms and prune back the rest, leaving two or three buds for renewal spurs; tie each arm along a horizontal wire.

Maggie Oster

Harvest grapes after their seeds turn brown.

angled outward. Staple no. 9 wire to posts. Most grapes should be planted 8 to 10 feet apart in the row, with rows 10 to 11 feet apart. Plant the vine at the same depth it grew in the nursery, and prune it back to a single stem, three buds tall.

When should I harvest my grapes?

Color is a poor indicator of grape ripeness. Some people judge simply by taste, but the seeds are also good measures: Green seeds mean unripe grapes; brown seeds show maturity. Always use shears to snip off fruit, rather than pulling it off the vines.

Can you suggest some grape varieties to try?

Good early varieties are Himrod and Interlaken Seedless; midseason varieties are Catawba, Concord, Fredonia, and Niagara; a popular late-season variety is Delaware.

Raspberries and Blackberries (*Rubus*)

What is the difference between raspberries and blackberries?

There are red, yellow, purple, and black raspberries and three types of blackberries, recognizable by growing habits. Cultivated blackberries tend to be less hardy than raspberries. Raspberries do best in the North and East, while blackberries are fine in more temperate climates. Raspberries tend to be more delicate and less seedy than blackberries. Some excellent red raspberries include the everbearers Fallred, September, and Southland; the midseason Newburgh; the early Sunrise; and the late Taylor. A good variety for the North is New Heritage. Some popular varieties of black raspberries are the early Allen and New Logan, the midseason Bristol and Cumberland, and the late Blackhawk and Morrison. An excellent blackberry variety is Darrow.

Do raspberries and blackberries need a lot of care?

They are among the easiest plants to grow. If plantings are well cared for, they may produce good crops for ten years or more. Most are seldom bothered by pests or diseases.

What kind of soil do raspberries and blackberries need?

Red raspberries prefer a neutral to alkaline soil of no lower pH than 6.0. Blackberries tolerate a more acid soil, between pH 5.0 and 6.0. Blackberries need a large supply of moisture as they grow and ripen, but the area must also be well drained. The fall before you plan to plant raspberries, prepare the area by digging in lime, compost, and commercial dried sheep manure and plant a cover crop of rye. The following spring, as soon as the soil can be worked, turn under the rye; do not fertilize at this time. Do not plant if the soil is excessively wet. If winters are not too severe in your region, red raspberries may be planted in the fall.

How do I plant raspberries and blackberries?

Cut back the tops of blackberries to about 2 inches. Set plants about 2 feet apart. Cut a slit in the soil with the blade of the shovel, then put the plant roots in the hole, setting the plant so that it is about the same depth as it was in the nursery. Firm soil around the root with your heel. Water heavily immediately after planting and every two days for the following two weeks. Mulch heavily.

How are raspberries and blackberries pruned?

After harvest cut down all canes that bore fruit that year; remove and burn these canes. Cut new canes to stand 4 feet tall. Wear thick gloves for this chore. In the spring you may wish to do further thinning to remove weak canes and to allow better air circulation and ease of picking.

How should I harvest raspberries and blackberries?

Reds are best when they are a deep garnet and begin to push away from the stem. Pick blackberries as soon as they become sweet, not necessarily when they first turn black; fruit should be fully ripened but firm. Pick both varieties often. Blackberries do not spoil as quickly if picked in the morning as when picked in the afternoon. Both are delicate and perishable; place them in small baskets so that they aren't crushed, and never press them down. Keep picked berries in the shade, and move them in to cool storage as soon as possible.

Harvest red raspberries when the fruit begins to push away from the stem, and move the picked fruit into a cool place as soon as possible.

Ron West

Strawberries *(Fragaria* spp.)

What is the difference between June-bearing and everbearing strawberries?

June-bearing strawberries produce one crop per year, in June. Everbearing types produce in spring, and then again in late-summer. A third type, called day-neutral, produces a heavy June crop, and then continues to produce smaller amounts of berries throughout the summer. The June-bearing types are a good choice for those who want a large crop all at once for canning, freezing, or preserving, while the everbearers and day-neutrals are good for those who don't want a big rush of strawberries all at once. The day-neutrals make wonderful hanging-basket plants, because they produce berries on the ends of their runners. Most strawberry lovers plant at least two kinds.

Can I grow strawberries in North Dakota?

You should be able to. Strawberries grow in Zones 3 through 10, though winter protection (mulching) is needed in colder climates. Selection of a suitable variety for your climate is of great importance, and not difficult since there are so many varieties available, both at garden centers and by mail.

What kind of soil should I provide for strawberries?

Strawberries grow best in fairly rich, slightly acid soil (pH 5 to 6) that is high in organic matter and well drained. Raised beds (see page 59) are a good idea where the soil is too heavy to drain well. Give strawberries full sun, and avoid planting them in low spots where frost collects. Prepare your soil by incorporating into it well-rotted, or dry, manure and great amounts of organic material at least a season ahead of planting time (preferably in the spring, although fall is acceptable).

What is the technique for planting strawberries?

Container-grown plants can go directly into planting holes with their root balls intact. If you are planting bare-rooted plants, soak them in water as you lay out the planting bed, then arrange them in any configuration, so long as the plants are 12 inches apart. Rows are usually 18 inches apart. Water the bed immediately after planting.

Will I be able to harvest strawberries the first year they are planted?

Not June-bearing varieties. Pinch off the first blossoms on both June-bearing and everbearing varieties. The everbearers will produce blossoms again for a late summer crop, but you will

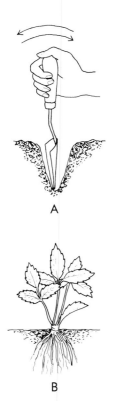

A

B

To plant strawberries, (A) make a hole by inserting the blade of a trowel straight into the soil, then pressing it back and forth and tipping it to both sides. Next, (B) set plant so that the base of the crown is at the level of the soil surface; spread out the roots; carefully firm the soil around them, leaving no air pockets in the soil; water well.

The second year after planting, remove enough of the new plants that have formed on runners, leaving 6 to 8 inches between remaining plants.

In order to encourage vigorous plant growth, remove blossom stems on first-year plants as soon as they appear.

have to wait for the second year for June-bearers. Also pinch off runners from both types the first year. These practices help the plants establish themselves for better crops in later seasons. The second year after planting, leave enough runners on the plants to allow them to reproduce themselves without overcrowding the bed. Once the plants are 6 to 8 inches apart in the beds, pinch off all runners.

Should I fertilize my strawberry bed?

A constant mulch of compost or well-rotted manure will probably provide adequate fertilization. Add a modest amount of nitrogen if, after the plants have been bearing for a while, the leaves are pale.

Should I water my strawberry bed?

Strawberries need to be kept moist in a well-drained soil. Compost, straw, or manure mulch will help. For best results in dry climates, use soaker hose or a drip-irrigation system.

How are strawberries harvested?

Once the plants begin to produce, pick the ripe berries every day, stems intact. Refrigerate them until you eat them, and do eat them soon—strawberries don't keep well.

Birds have been the greatest pests of my berries. How can I keep them away?

Plastic netting suspended over supports will keep them from damaging your crop.

Are there many insect pests of strawberries?

Earwigs, slugs, and snails are big problems in some areas. You may also be bothered by Japanese beetles, aphids, thrips, weevils, nematodes, and mites. See pages 19 and 85-90 for controls.

Pick ripe strawberries daily, keeping their stems intact.

Selected Varieties of Strawberries

NAME	FRUIT DESCRIPTION	PLANT CHARACTERISTICS
Allstar	Large, firm, light red fruits with mild, sweet flesh	June-bearing; productive; disease-resistant
Cardinal	Very large, bright red, firm, sweet fruits	June-bearing; bears abundantly; vigorous; disease-resistant except for verticillium wilt; good for the North, but will do well in Zone 8 also
Earliglow	Large, deep red, glossy, sweet berries	June-bearing; vigorous and productive; resistant to verticillium wilt, leaf spot, and leaf scorch; good in mid-Atlantic, Northeast, and North Central regions; Zones 4-8
Guardian	Very large, glossy, light red, firm berries	June-bearing; later than Surecrop, but more resistant to disease; ripens midseason; Zones 4-8
Ozark Beauty	Large, bright red, long-necked, firm fruits	Everbearing; highly productive; hardy; bears from late spring through September; adaptable to variety of soils; good in the North and Southern mountains; Zones 4-8
Red Chief	Medium to large, glossy, red berries	June-bearing; resistant to root rot; productive; good in Northeast to North Carolina and Illinois
Sparkle	Dark red berries	June-bearing; vigorous; hardy; disease-resistant except for verticillium wilt; good in Northeast to Maryland and Illinois
Surecrop	Large, deep red, glossy, slightly tart berries	June-bearing; productive; disease-resistant; good choice for beginners; good for North and Central United States; Zones 4-8
Tristar	Medium-sized, glossy, deep red, sweet fruits	Day-neutral; highly disease-resistant; runners set fruit even before they take root; good in hanging basket; Zones 5-8

What are the diseases of strawberries?

Verticillium wilt is the principal disease problem. It is best controlled by purchasing certified disease-free plants and rotating crops every three to four years. Root rot is preventable with proper planting depth and well-drained beds. Leaf spot, a fungus disease, can be prevented by providing good air circulation and by planting resistant varieties.

I don't have much room, but I would love to grow strawberries. Is it possible to grow them in containers?

A very attractive way of raising strawberries is to grow them in a barrel. Cut four 1-inch drainage holes in the bottom of a barrel. Cut additional 2-inch holes in the sides of the barrel, spaced about 1 foot apart horizontally and 8 inches apart vertically. Fill the bottom of the barrel with 6 inches of gravel, for drainage. Form a chicken-wire cylinder, 4 inches wide and as long as the barrel is high. Place the cylinder in the center of the barrel and fill it with gravel. For your soil mixture, use equal parts of rich garden loam, compost, and vermiculite or sand.

To set the plants, pour in enough soil mixture on top of the gravel to reach the bottom of the first row of planting holes. Carefully push the strawberry roots through the hole from the outside in, and, making sure that the roots point downward rather than sideward, push them into the soil. Add more soil and gently firm the plants into place. Fill all of the bottom row of holes, before adding more soil to bring the soil level up to the next row of holes. Continue planting in this manner until all holes are filled. When the barrel is filled, add three or four plants to the top. Water thoroughly. See pages 83-85 for directions on the care of container plants.

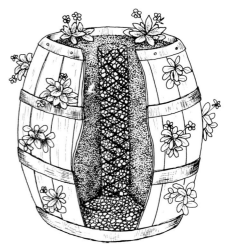

A barrel makes a convenient and attractive planter for growing an abundance of strawberries in a small space.

4 *Your Home Vegetable Garden*

Raising vegetables can be one of the most satisfying kinds of gardening. Nothing purchased at the store can ever quite match the tender, crisp, sweet freshness of vegetables rushed from the garden to the table. Of all the plants one can grow, vegetables are among the easiest to nurture and the quickest to reach maturity. And, as if these were not assets enough, vegetable plants are often quite beautiful: Witness the ruffles and frills of lettuces and kale, the hearty gleam of tomatoes and peppers, the feathery grace of carrots and asparagus. Well-tended beds filled with the many textures and hues of vegetables and framed by neatly mulched straw paths earn a place of pride in any landscape. To achieve such a goal, all that is needed is thoughtful planning and careful nurture of the soil and the young plants growing in it.

What climatic factors should I consider when planning my vegetable garden?

Begin by determining whether the hardiness zone where you live (see pages 1-2) is suitable for the vegetable variety you wish to grow. Next, ask yourself some questions about your own location within the general hardiness zone: Do you live at the top or the bottom of a hill? Frost comes earlier to valleys than to high places, because cold air runs downhill at night and collects in "pools," just like water does. Is there a lot of wind where you live? Wind lowers ambient temperatures, creating the "chill factor" that makes you pull your coat tightly around you on

SELECTING THE SITE

•

♦ *Nothing purchased at the supermarket can ever quite match the crisp, sweet freshness of vegetables straight from the garden.*

53

blustery days. Do you live in a deep, narrow valley, where the summer sun can be very intense? The direct rays of the sun can burn tender plant leaves, as well as heat the soil to harmfully high temperatures. All these factors contribute to micro-climates—the combined effects of weather and geographical conditions from acre to acre and plot to plot. Because of micro-climates where you garden, you may be able to grow a wider variety of vegetables and fruits than you might have first imagined.

What is the best climate for growing vegetables?

Fortunately for gardeners spread out across the continent, there is no single area in which one must live to enjoy great vegetable gardening success. Some vegetables, such as *Brassicas* (cabbage, broccoli, and Brussels sprouts, for example) prefer cool weather without intense sunlight, while others, such as tomatoes, peppers, eggplants, and melons, require hot, sunny weather. With care, you can grow vegetables for which your climate seems unsuitable. No matter where you live, however, you will find that there are certain vegetables that thrive in your particular climate.

How much sunlight does a vegetable garden need?

Your garden needs full sunlight at least five or six hours a day. If you have no sunny spot, you could create one by pruning back or removing a tree or hedge. Grow vegetables in your front yard, if necessary; a well-kept vegetable garden can only enhance the beauty of a front landscape.

Are there any vegetables that I can grow in the shade?

Lettuce needs at least a half day of full, though not intense, sunlight, but it actually benefits from midday shade. Asparagus and rhubarb will tolerate shade after their growth in early spring. Cucumbers do well in partial shade. Vegetables that survive with minimal sunlight (five to six hours per day) are beets, carrots, cauliflower, radishes, spinach, and Swiss chard.

How close to a large maple tree can I plant my vegetable garden?

Plant it no closer than the outer reaches of the tree's branches, and preferably a few feet farther away than that. Trees too close to a garden will rob the plants of nutrients and water, as well as sunlight.

I have no flat areas in my yard. Is there any way I can have a vegetable garden?

Terrace otherwise-useless slopes with heavy timber or stone walls, filled in with topsoil. Plant vegetables that need the warmest, sunniest conditions on the highest terraces, with more cold-tolerant varieties toward the bottom, where chill temperatures or even late spring or early frosts may settle.

If I don't have a southern exposure for my garden bed, am I at a real disadvantage?

Although southern exposures warm up fastest in the spring, northern exposures are good for growing cool-weather crops such as lettuce and peas. There is no one perfect exposure.

On my small lot, I have little choice about where my vegetable garden will be. Is there any way that I can modify the climate where my garden must be placed?

Yes. Even if an ideal site is unavailable, you can improve weather conditions with the addition of windbreaks, shade-giving structures or plants, mulches (pages 77-78), and irrigation practices (pages 78-80).

What size garden should I start out with?

This depends on how much space you have available, how much produce you want from your garden, and how much work you are willing to put into it. A modest-sized, 10-by-20-foot plot is quite manageable in terms of weeding, cultivating, planting, harvesting, and, in dry climates, irrigating. Even a 10-by-10-foot plot will give you plenty of room for a salad, or "kitchen," garden, which will supply you with greens and herbs for salads

A 10-by-20-foot garden is easy to manage and produces a great variety and quantity of food for a family.

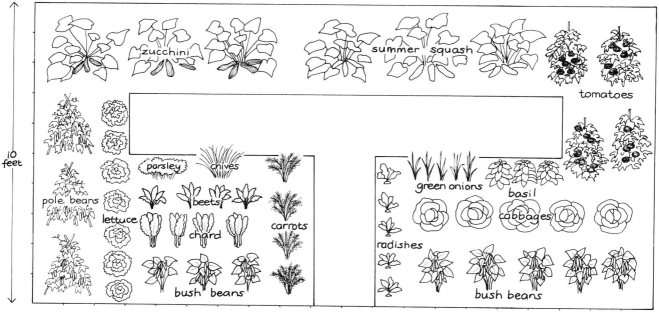

and seasonings on a daily basis. Kitchen gardens traditionally feature lettuce, radishes, tomatoes, peppers, scallions, and herbs. If you want to start more slowly or if you have very limited space, plant vegetables in containers (see pages 83-85).

WHAT SHALL I GROW?

How can I know which vegetables will do best in my area?

Begin by asking your gardening neighbors and friends, as well as local gardening clubs and your county Extension Service agent, who is intimately acquainted with local growing conditions and is thus an extremely valuable source of information and encouragement. (County Extension Services are branches of the U.S. Department of Agriculture, and often associated with the state university.) Many catalogues provide detailed planting instructions for each variety listed, and seed houses often offer free advice over the telephone to anyone with a question.

SHORT-SEASON CROPS

Arugula
Beans (bush)
Beets
Cabbage, early (including Chinese)
Carrots
Lettuce
Mustard greens
Onions (from sets)
Peas
Radishes
Scallions
Turnips

What vegetables shall I grow in my small garden?

Here are three good guidelines to follow: Plant the vegetables you and your family like to eat; plant crops that do well in your area; and decide whether you wish to grow crops for fresh use only, or also for freezing, storing, drying, and canning. To get the most out of limited space, plant short-season crops (those that mature rapidly) and follow them in the same spot by another crop of the same or a different vegetable. See the chart on this page for suggestions.

What are the most productive crops?

In space, as well as the time it takes to grow them, the most productive vegetables are tomatoes, followed in order by bush beans, broccoli, onions (from sets; see page 119), beets, carrots, Swiss chard, Chinese cabbage, New Zealand spinach, mustard greens, lettuce, turnips, cabbage, radishes, spinach, and bush (summer) squash.

LONG-SEASON CROPS

Artichokes
Asparagus
Beans (dry, lima, and soy)
Celery
Eggplant
Kale
Leeks
Onions
Peppers
Potatoes
Rhubarb
Tomatoes

What are the easiest crops to grow?

Try tomatoes, beans (green and dry), beets, lettuce, potatoes, radishes, most root crops, salad greens, squash (summer and winter), sunflowers, and Swiss chard.

What are the more challenging crops to grow?

In most areas, that list includes cantaloupe, cauliflower, celery, Chinese cabbage, corn, leeks, parsnips, peas, and watermelon.

CROPS THAT GROW BEST IN COOL WEATHER

Artichokes, Jerusalem
Arugula
Asparagus
Beans, broad (fava)
Beets
Broccoli
Brussels sprouts
Cabbage (including Chinese)
Carrots
Cauliflower

Celery
Chicory
Collards*
Endive
Kale
Kohlrabi
Leeks
Lettuce
Mustard greens
Onions

Parsnips
Peas
Potatoes
Radicchio
Radishes
Rhubarb
Rutabagas
Swiss chard*
Shallots
Spinach
Turnips

* Will also grow well in hot weather

CROPS THAT GROW BEST IN WARM WEATHER

Artichokes, globe
Beans (except fava)
Corn
Cowpeas (blackeyed peas)
Cucumbers

Eggplant
Lima beans
Melons
Okra
Peppers

Pumpkins
Soybeans
Spinach, New Zealand
Squash, summer and winter
Sweet potatoes
Tomatoes

What is the purpose of a garden journal?

This can be as fancy or as simple as you like. It should include a map of your garden and a record of what you have planted where, and the date. You may wish to record your impressions of how well or how poorly certain varieties have fared from one year to the next, your smashing successes and regrettable failures—and the way you'll do things next time, now that you know better.

Should my planting rows run north and south or east and west?

More important than compass orientation, a garden's rows (or rectangular planting beds) should run *along* a slope rather than up and down it, and tall-growing plants should not shade other plants.

What other things should I consider when laying out my garden plan?

Be sure to leave room to move around and to bring in equipment, such as a wheelbarrow or garden hose. It's nice, if possible, to have the garden close enough to the kitchen so that you won't hesitate to run out and pluck a few leaves of this or that while the pots boil.

DECIDING ON A GARDEN PLAN

SPACE REQUIREMENTS OF VEGETABLES

Least Space-Consuming

Beans (bush and pole)
Beets
Carrots
Chinese cabbage
Eggplant
Leeks
Lettuce
Mustard greens
Onions
Parsnips
Peppers
Radishes
Sunflowers
Swiss chard
Tomatoes
Turnips

Most Space-Consuming

Artichoke (globe)
Broccoli
Cauliflower
Corn
Cucumbers
Melons
Peas
Potatoes
Sweet potatoes
Winter squash

Vegetables planted in wide rows, as shown here, benefit from the warm, moist microclimate created by the beds.

What are the advantages of growing vegetables in beds rather than in rows?

If you plant in single rows, a path will run between each row and most of your garden will be devoted to paths rather than vegetables. When vegetables are planted in beds (wide rows), they benefit from the warm, moist microclimate created by the beds and their roots are removed from the dry, compacted soil of the paths. If you plant in permanent beds year after year, you never fertilize ground that will in the future be walked upon, and

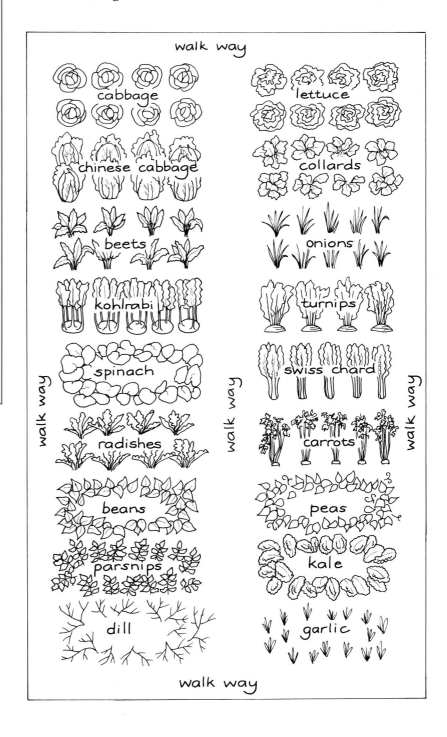

you never walk upon and compress soil that will in the future support plants. Furthermore, if you make each of your permanent beds equal to 100 square feet (5 by 20 feet, or 4 by 25, for example), you will be able to compute fertilizer needs quite simply. Permanent beds tend to turn into raised beds as you add soil amendments over the seasons.

How are raised beds made?

Remove the topsoil from the areas where the paths between the beds will be, and add it to the beds. Or, bring in enough soil-building material to bring up the beds to their proper height—4 to 12 inches higher than the surrounding soil.

Mark the site of the bed by hammering in stakes at the corners and connecting the stakes with string to define the sides. The bed should be no wider than 40 to 48 inches, so that you can easily reach the center from either side. Make the paths about 16 to 24 inches wide. Dig the soil to a depth of about 10 inches, working from the center of the bed out to the sides. Add topsoil from the paths to the bed and work that in as you dig. This is the time, too, to incorporate compost or other organic material, if you wish. Allow the freshly dug bed to settle and dry in the sun for a few days, and then lightly rake soil up from the edges of the bed to the center and flatten the bed with the back of the rake to level it. Some gardeners build wooden frames around their raised beds to hold the soil in place, but this isn't usually necessary, and may, in fact, encourage insect pests such as slugs to take up residence in your garden. The best material for framing is cedar or redwood, both of which resist rot.

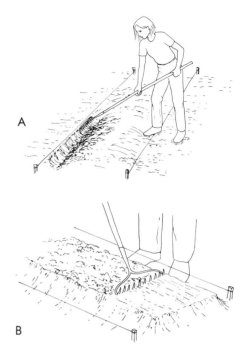

A

B

Form raised beds by (A) raking about 4 to 6 inches of topsoil from the path onto the bed and (B) smoothing the top of the bed with the back of the rake.

In an established raised-bed garden, you never fertilize ground that will in the future be walked upon, and you never walk upon and compress soil that will in the future support plants.

Martha Storey

PREPARING THE SOIL

What do gardeners mean when they say, "Plants don't like to have wet feet"?

Ideally, water should drain gradually through the topsoil, into the subsoil, and then into the water table, without staying in one place for a long time and causing waterlogged roots. If puddles stay on the ground several hours after a hard rain, the ground is poorly drained. Heavy clay soils can hold water for so long that the roots of plants growing in it become deprived of oxygen, and the plants actually drown. Extremely sandy or gravelly soils, on the other hand, don't hold water long enough. The water passes by the roots so quickly that the plants are not able to take in enough moisture, and they die of thirst.

What can I do about a soil that holds water for too long?

The first step is to add plenty of organic matter, such as manure or compost, which will help loosen and aerate the soil. You can also plant a green manure crop (see page 61) and then till it in. Gypsum, available at nurseries, will help break up a heavy clay soil. Make certain never to work a heavy clay soil when it is wet, or you will break down the soil structure and cause it to dry in cementlike clods that will be almost impossible to break up. If the water problem is severe, build raised beds on top of the ground and fill them with a 50/50 blend of topsoil and peat moss.

What should I do about sandy soil that won't hold water?

Mix great amounts of organic material into the soil each fall, and again in the spring. Peat moss is especially good for sandy or gravelly soils, because it holds many times its weight in water. Begin by mixing it into the top 4 inches of soil; each year, as you add more, you can dig it in a little deeper. If your soil is little more than sand, you might consider purchasing good-quality topsoil from a reputable nursery. Be sure to add organic matter even to purchased topsoil.

Is a soil test necessary?

Not always. Your Extension Service agent or a knowledgeable nursery person can tell you much about the soil in your region, and what the gardeners in your area add to their soil for optimum growing conditions.

Should I add lime to my soil?

Lime needs vary greatly throughout North America. In some areas the soil is alkaline rather than acid, in which case lime would only make conditions worse. Contact your Extension Service agent, who will know whether lime is needed in your area.

What is green manure?

Green manure is a cover crop, such as buckwheat, grown to be dug back into the soil to increase soil fertility and improve soil texture. Green manure crops are beneficial even on gardens as small as 10 by 25 feet. Check with your Extension Service agent for suggestions of what are the best crops to use in your area.

Won't a green manure crop turn into a weed problem?

Not if you turn it under *before* it produces mature seeds. Green manure can actually be used as an aid *against* weed problems (see pages 76-77).

What is humus?

Humus is decomposed animal or vegetable matter, available from such sources as well-rotted manure, peat moss, seaweed, leaf mold, and compost. It acts as a sponge, holding water and oxygen in the soil; protects soil from erosion by water and wind; improves the texture of hard clay soil by separating it into smaller clumps; stabilizes the soil chemically, buffering your plants against fertilizer burn; and makes nutrients more available to plants. Some gardeners say that the difference between "dirt" and "soil" is humus.

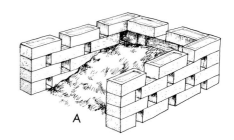

Compost

How can I make my own compost?

Simply combine rough organic matter, soil, and moisture with a high-nitrogen substance, such as fertilizer, blood meal, fresh manure, or cottonseed meal. As the compost pile decomposes, it heats up and changes in character from a mixture of, for example, manure, kitchen scraps, garden soil, leaves, grass clippings, and blood meal into the light, sweet-smelling, almost fluffy material known as compost.

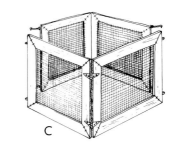

How big can my compost heap be?

A good workable size is 4 feet by 4 feet, and no more than 4 feet high. You can buy a ready-made unit or make your own.

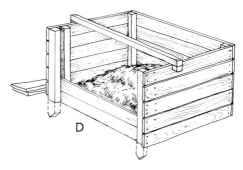

Can composting be done in a trash barrel?

Yes—or even in plastic trash bags. Mix your materials well, moisten them, and fill your barrel or bags and seal them. They may be ready in three weeks in warm weather or two months in cool weather.

Compost bins can be simply made with (A) concrete blocks, (B) fencing, (C) a frame made of 1x6s and 1-inch wire mesh, or (D) a sturdy box with a removable front and a bar across the top to prevent spreading.

How can I make sure my compost pile heats up?

Add plenty of nitrogen, stir the heap every week or so to incorporate oxygen (by sinking pipes into the compost and rocking them in a circular motion), and make sure the heap never dries out—it should be moist but not soggy.

Can I compost in the winter?

Where the ground freezes, no composting action will occur until there is a thaw, and even in milder areas, very little composting will take place during the winter. If you continue to add kitchen scraps, leaves, lawn clippings, and soil, however, as soon as the weather warms up, your pile will begin to "work," or heat up.

How hot will a compost heap get? Is there danger of fire?

The more nitrogen you add, the faster your compost heap will heat up and, to a point, the hotter it will become. It should reach 150° F. Piles do occasionally smolder, so don't put yours next to a house, tree, or anything that could catch fire.

How do I keep the pile from smelling unpleasant?

If you add fresh manure or kitchen scraps, cover it with dirt or dried clippings to keep odors and flies at bay.

Can I add tree and bush prunings to my compost heap?

Thick, unshredded, woody material takes longer to break down, and is therefore best not added. As a rule of thumb, don't add anything that you can't easily break up with the edge of a shovel.

Will seeds from grass clippings and weeds stay in my compost and later sprout in my garden?

If your compost pile heats up to 150° F. (you can check it with an oven thermometer), all weed seeds will be destroyed. Turning your pile occasionally ensures that everything in it gets heated up.

Is there anything I shouldn't add to my compost heap?

In addition to woody material such as branches and thick twigs, avoid magnolia leaves, which don't break down easily; eucalyptus, which contains an oil that is detrimental to plant growth; and any plants that are noxious weeds or implacable spreaders (morning glory, English ivy, Bermuda grass, and nut grass are examples). Also avoid meat scraps. Anything that might attract animals to an unenclosed compost heap should be buried deeply in the heap.

Digging the Garden

When is the best time to work the soil?

Dig in the fall, and leave the ground rough. Freezing and thawing during winter breaks up clods and aerates the soil, insect enemies that might otherwise have overwintered in the soil will be turned out, and settling will lessen the likelihood of air pockets in the soil when planting. One exception: Light, sandy soils, which can suffer from erosion by winter rains, are usually best tilled in the spring.

Must I use a power tiller, or will a spade do?

If you have a large garden—particularly if it is presently in sod—you will find a rotary power tiller immensely helpful. You can usually hire someone to come and do this for you or you can rent equipment if you don't wish to purchase it. On the other hand, some people enjoy turning over established gardens with a spade, and raised beds (see page 59) must be done this way. Work on a cool day, and take your time so that you don't strain unused muscles.

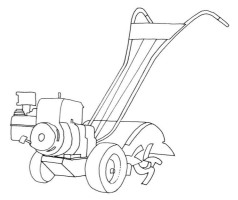

A rotary power tiller is helpful if you have a large garden to cultivate.

What if I didn't dig in the fall—can I dig in the spring?

Yes, but before you begin, make this simple test: Pick up a handful of soil and squeeze it into a ball. If the ball breaks up easily, the soil is ready to be dug. If the ball is sticky and elastic, and retains its shape under pressure, the soil is still too moist to be dug.

Is there more I should do in the spring if I have tilled and fertilized and added compost to the soil in the fall?

For best results, add more organic matter to the soil in the spring a week or two before planting. Spread compost, aged manure, or other bulky, organic, soil-building material 2 to 4 inches deep on top of the soil, and dig it in to a depth of 12 inches.

Is it enough to turn over the soil at spade depth, or do I need to dig down really deeply?

Some gardeners favor the double-digging method devised by French intensive gardeners (see illustration). In deeply dug gardens, plant roots find it easier to reach down in search of water and nutrients. The result is plants that are healthier, better able to ward off insects, compete with weeds, and withstand dry spells, and thus a garden that does not need as much attention as a shallowly dug one. In most dry locations (except for some sandy soils) it is especially necessary to encourage roots to strike deeply in search of moisture.

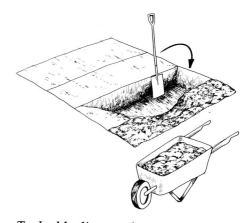

To double-dig a garden, remove one row of soil (a shovel's width and depth) from one end of the garden and place it in a wheelbarrow. Loosen the exposed subsoil a shovel's depth. Cover the exposed subsoil with the top layer of the next row of soil (as shown by arrow), and loosen the newly exposed subsoil a shovel's depth. Continue down the bed in this manner, using the reserved soil from the wheelbarrow to fill the final trench.

Fertilizing

What is the difference between organic and inorganic fertilizers?

The former are made from animal, vegetable, or mineral sources, such as bonemeal, blood meal, or cottonseed meal, and rock phosphates; the latter are made from treated minerals (such as superphosphate, nitrate salts, or potash salts) or extracted from the air (ammonium forms of nitrogen).

What are the advantages of natural fertilizers?

Perhaps the greatest advantage is that they encourage beneficial life forms in the soil rather than harming them, as some commercial dry fertilizers can. Many of the natural fertilizers build soil structure by adding valuable bulky organic-matter that increases the humus content of the soil. Natural fertilizers also add minor nutrients, which are less well understood than N, P, and K (see page 66), but vital to the health of all plants. Furthermore, they release their nutrients slowly, which is the safest way to fertilize.

What are the disadvantages of natural fertilizers?

Some people object to the odor of manures and fish emulsions, though some dry commercial brands are deodorized. Because many natural fertilizers contain a great deal of soil-building organic material, they can be difficult to transport, and more time-consuming to apply. The nutrient content of most natural fertilizers is not as easy to determine as it is for commercial fertilizers.

What are the advantages of commercial fertilizers?

They contain nutrients in precise amounts, so that you know exactly what you're applying. In addition, they are less bulky than natural fertilizers such as manure or compost, they act quickly, and they are usually less expensive than store-bought natural fertilizers in terms of the amount of N, P, and K that they provide per dollar.

What are the disadvantages of commercial dry fertilizers?

They add no soil-building organic matter to the soil. Soils supplemented with commercial dry fertilizers and nothing else tend actually to die—that is, earthworms disappear, soil microbes and enzymes die or stop working, and the soil breaks down and loses its structure, with erosion the result. Fast-acting synthetic fertilizers have some other risks. If you add too much at once, your plants will be burned by salts in the fertilizer, and soils enriched with these fertilizers must be fertilized more often than soils enriched with slow-releasing natural fertilizers.

Percentage Composition
of Common Organic Materials

	NITROGEN	PHOSPHORUS	POTASSIUM
Activated sludge	5.00	3.00	
Alfalfa hay	2.45	.50	2.10
Animal tankage	8.00	20.00	
Apple leaves	1.00	.15	.35
Basic slag	.80		
Blood meal	15.00	1.30	.70
Bonemeal	4.00	21.00	.20
Brewer's grains (wet)	.90	.50	.05
Castor pomace	5.50	1.50	1.25
Cattle manure (fresh)	.29	.17	.35
Cocoa shell dust	1.04	1.49	2.71
Coffee grounds (dried)	1.99	.36	.67
Colloidal phosphate		18-24	
Cornstalks	.75	.40	.90
Cottonseed	3.15	1.25	1.15
Cottonseed hull ash		8.70	24.00
Cottonseed meal	7.00	2.50	1.50
Dried blood	12-15	3.00	
Feather meal	12.00		
Fish scrap (red snapper)	7.76	13.00	3.80
Granite dust			5.00
Greensand		1.50	5.00
Guano	12.00	8.00	3.00
Hoof meal and horn dust	12.50	1.75	
Horse manure (fresh)	.44	.17	.35
Incinerator ash	.24	5.15	2.33
Leather dust	5.5-12		
Oak leaves	.80	.35	.15
Peach leaves	.90	.15	.60
Phosphate rock		30-32	
Poultry manure (fresh)	2.00	1.88	1.85
Rabbit manure (fresh)	2.40	.62	.05
Red clover	.55	.13	.50
Seaweed	1.68	.75	5.00
Sheep manure (fresh)	.55	.31	.15
Swine manure (fresh)	.60	.41	.13
Tankage	6.00	8.00	
Tobacco stems	2.00		7.00
Wood ashes		1.50	7.00

What do the numbers on the fertilizer bags mean?

They give the percentages of the most important plant nutrients: nitrogen (N), phosphorus (P), and potassium (K), always in that order. A bag of fertilizer with the formula 5-10-5 contains by volume 5-percent nitrogen, 10-percent phosphorus, and 5-percent potassium. The remaining 80 percent is some kind of filler—usually organic matter that will increase the humus content of your soil.

What is "organic gardening"?

In general, to garden organically is to add only mineral-, plant-, and animal-derived materials to the soil and plants, and to refrain from using chemical pesticides or herbicides. Both aspects—adding nutrients *and* avoiding chemicals—are crucial to the success of this method.

Should I use both commercial dry fertilizers and manure?

If you garden organically, aged and composted manure, followed by sidedressings of compost and cottonseed or blood meal, once your plants get going, should be enough. The commercial fertilizer equivalent of this would be a 5-10-5 mixture.

What does the term "complete fertilizer" mean?

This term is misleading, for such a product sometimes contains only the three major nutrients (N, P, and K), and these three are far from a complete list of plant nutrients. The closest thing to a truly complete fertilizer is compost, which you can make yourself (see pages 61-62).

What is "plant food"?

The primary "food" for plants is sunlight. It is better to think in terms of feeding the *soil* rather than feeding the *plants* growing in it. Healthy soil contains not only nitrogen, phosphorus, and potassium, but microbiotic life forms, oxygen, earthworms, enzymes, trace elements, and many other things that contribute to the health of plants.

When should I add commercial fertilizer to the soil?

Spread it over the soil before you begin digging so that you can work it into the soil as you dig.

What is a "starter" or "transplanting" fertilizer?

This consists of a small amount of a powerful fertilizer, high in phosphorus (such as bonemeal, phosphate rock, or superphosphate), dissolved in water. Pour a cupful around the plants when they are transplanted, or pour a cupful directly on the seed for every 3 feet of row. An ounce of 13-26-13 fertilizer, or 3 ounces of a 5-10-5 fertilizer dissolved in a gallon of water, are typical starter solutions.

What is a "sidedressing" fertilizer?

A sidedressing is applied to a plant once it is growing. Heavy feeders such as corn and cabbage family crops benefit in particular from additional small applications of fertilizers between the time they are planted and the harvest. Leaves streaked with yellow are a signal that a sidedressing may be needed.

What should I use for a sidedressing?

Compost or dried manure spread 1 inch deep around each plant, or to either side of a row of plants, and then raked in, makes a good sidedressing. Manure or compost "tea" (made by soaking the material overnight in a bucket of water) is also effective. Or you can use 1 tablespoon of dry commercial fertilizer per plant or two or three parts fertilizer to one part water. Water the fertilizer in immediately. Plants with high nitrogen needs, such as corn, should be sidedressed with a high-nitrogen fertilizer.

Is there much difference in various animal manures?

Poultry manure, much higher in nitrogen than steer or horse manure, should be aged at least nine months and used in smaller quantities. Aged horse manure is an excellent soil builder and conditioner: Spread about 3 inches of it across the top of the soil before you dig. Nitrogen content is sometimes written on the package label of commercial dry manures. Refer to the chart on page 65 if you have a local source of animal manures.

Is it necessary to age fresh manure before using it?

Yes, both to keep it from burning plants and to kill the weed seeds in it.

Do some types of vegetables have special fertilizer needs?

Leafy vegetables, such as lettuce, Swiss chard, and cabbage, use large amounts of nitrogen. Seed- or fruit-producing vegetables, such as beans and tomatoes, use much potassium. See Chapter 6 for more information on individual crop needs.

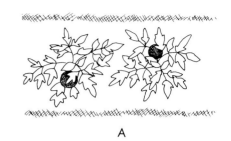

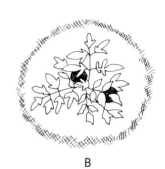

Sidedressing fertilizers may be applied (A) along both sides of a row of plants or (B) in a circle around plants.

5 *Planting and Growing Vegetables*

I t seems a shame to let those first spring days of warmth and sunshine pass by without starting something growing, yet if seeds are planted outdoors too soon, a late frost can put your work to waste. That's why it's a good idea to start seeds in containers, flats, or cold frames before dependable gardening weather arrives. This way you not only have something to relieve that persistent gardening itch, but you will reap your rewards much sooner in the form of early crops.

How soon should I start seeds indoors?

As a rule, start seeds eight weeks before you would plant them outside. See the entries for individual vegetables in Chapter 6 for more precise guidelines.

What are seed flats?

Traditional seed flats are simply small, open, well-drained wooden boxes, easily built out of redwood or cedar scraps. A good size is 12 by 24 inches and no less than 3 inches deep. If you plan to keep seedlings in the flats for six weeks or longer, make the flats 6 inches deep so that roots have more room. Leave ⅛-inch spaces between the slats on the bottom so that the soil can drain easily.

You can also start seeds in cottage cheese containers, cut-off milk cartons, margarine tubs, foam or paper cups, or yogurt containers, with several holes poked in the bottoms of them for

STARTING SEEDS IN FLATS

♦ *Seeds started indoors in flats or other containers will give you a head start on the gardening season.*

69

drainage. (Arrange them on a tray so that when the seedlings must be moved, the containers' shapes are not distorted and the root systems thus disturbed.) Seed catalogues and garden centers sell plastic trays with many individual cells, which make removal for transplanting easy. Some have plastic domes that fit snugly over them to create a warm, humid, greenhouselike atmosphere, especially conducive to germination.

Can I use garden soil in my starter flats?

Garden soil is too dense for optimum seed sprouting in flats. The best choice for indoor sprouting is a potting soil, available wherever garden supplies are sold. If you use sterilized soil, your plants will be less likely to suffer damping-off disease, which frequently causes young seedlings to die.

How much light should I give indoor-planted seeds?

Most seeds will sprout in the dark if they are warm enough, but once they're up they need a lot of light. Place them in a sunny window, but don't let intense sunlight dry out or overheat newly sprouted plants.

Will vegetable seedlings grow well under artificial light?

Yes. Fluorescent tubes, turned on fourteen hours a day, will provide plenty of light. You can supplement weak natural light by turning fluorescent lights on at 4 p.m. and off at 9 p.m. Suspend them 4 inches above the growing surface, and move them up as the plants grow so that they are always about 4 inches above the tops of the plants.

Fluorescent lights should be suspended about 4 inches above the growing surface of the plants and raised as the plants grow.

Should I thin vegetable seedlings in flats before transplanting them?

If you sow the seeds far enough apart in the flats, you won't have to do much thinning. If the little plants are crowded, however, thin them when they put out their first set of true leaves (the set of leaves that appears after the first leaves).

How deeply should I plant seeds in flats, trays, or containers?

As a general rule, plant them four times as deep as their diameter—the same depth at which you would plant them in the garden. Don't forget to label them!

How warm should the potting soil be?

For germination, provide 60° F. for hardy plants and 70° F. for tender ones. If you place heat cables or mats beneath seed flats or trays, remove them as soon as the seedlings are well up. Soil temperatures above 90° F. are harmful. After they are growing, hardy plants, such as members of the cabbage family, can withstand night temperatures of 40° to 50° F., though 60° F. would be better.

How should I water seeds sprouting in containers?

Use a plant mister or a watering can with a very fine-holed nozzle. Indoors, flats or containers can be watered from beneath by setting them in leakproof trays. This method assures that the seeds won't be uncovered and washed away. Sufficient, uninterrupted moisture is essential.

Since starting seeds in flats means that I will have to move plants into the garden, what are the best vegetables for transplanting?

All members of the cabbage family transplant well, as do tomatoes, eggplants, peppers, onions, leeks, lettuce, and celery. Melons and squashes should not remain in containers more than two or three weeks.

Which vegetables don't transplant well?

Parsnips, carrots, and other root crops don't respond well to transplanting, though beets are an exception if handled carefully. Beans and corn are best started in the ground because you need so many of them.

What is "hardening off"?

It is the process of acclimating indoor-grown seedlings to outdoor weather conditions so that they won't suffer transplant shock. Starting two weeks before transplanting, set your flats or containers outside during the daylight hours in a well-protected, partially shaded area. After three or four days, leave them out at night if you can be sure that it will not get too cold.

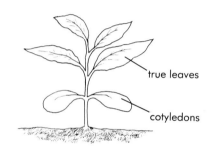

True leaves appear after the first seed leaves, or cotyledons.

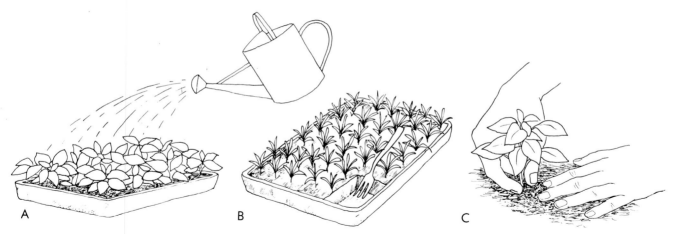

To transplant seedlings into the garden, (A) moisten plants before beginning. (B) Remove seedlings from flats by cutting out the block of soil on which they are growing. (C) Gently lower seedling into a prepared hole, watering the plant immediately and firming soil to settle soil around roots.

TRANSPLANTING SEEDLINGS INTO THE GARDEN

How should I go about transplanting?

Have your garden beds well prepared (see pages 60-67) before you do anything to your seedlings. Water the containers in which they are growing so that the soil is well moistened, but not soggy. If the seedlings are growing in a molded plastic "plug" tray, lift them out gently by the two strongest leaves, place them immediately in the furrow or holes you have dug, and firm the soil around them. Plants growing in individual containers can be removed by inverting the container into the palm of your hand. A rap on the bottom of the container is sometimes necessary to free the root ball. Seedlings growing in a flat need to be separated from each other before being removed from the flat. Use a hand fork, an old kitchen spatula, or a putty knife to cut the soil into blocks. When the roots of the individual seedlings are well separated in this fashion, lift them from the flat and plant them.

Should I water the plants after transplanting them?

Light watering immediately after transplanting is helpful. It is the gentlest way to settle soil around the roots. Do not tightly compress wet soil around the roots of transplanted seedlings.

DIRECT SEEDING

Direct seeding is the most common method of planting most vegetables. After you have prepared the soil thoroughly (see pages 60-67), rake it smooth and remove large stones, as you would before transplanting.

How should I direct-seed in rows?

Create shallow furrows with the edge of a hoe, drop in the seeds, cover them over with compost, leaf mold, or potting soil, tamp down the covering with the flat end of the hoe, and label what you've planted.

Is it always best to plant in furrows?

Not necessarily. You can plant in any pattern you like, as long as you provide adequate spacing for mature plants and leave yourself access to what you plant. Small kitchen gardens often feature curved rows, accent plantings of only two or three plants of one kind in one place, and geometrically shaped blocks of colorful vegetables (such as red- and green-leafed lettuces) interposed against each other.

Can you explain the meaning of a hill planting?

A hill is a cluster of plants as opposed to a row—it is not necessarily raised higher than the surrounding ground. Cucumbers, melons, pole beans, and squash are all often planted in hills.

What is a drill?

A drill is a very shallow seeding hole, such as you would poke with a finger or small stick.

Should I remove stones of all sizes from the planting bed before seeding?

No. The soil should be made up of many different-sized particles of dirt and stone, rather than fine as dust. Remove only stones that are large enough to prevent the emergence of a seedling or that occupy too much space in the garden bed.

When is the right time to plant seeds outdoors?

This depends on local conditions and on what you are planting. Check with your local Extension Service to find out the date of the last expected frost in your area. The lists on page 57 will help you determine which vegetables can go in the ground first, and which should be planted once the soil has warmed up.

How deeply should I plant seeds outdoors?

The same depth as indoors—roughly four times the diameter of the seed. Follow seed packet instructions for planting depth and spacing.

What is pelleted seed?

Some seed companies coat very small seeds with a nutrient substance to make them larger for easier planting and better germination. Pelleted seeds are always more expensive than uncoated seeds, and are sometimes available only in large quantities.

How does one broadcast seeds?

Gardeners with raised beds often broadcast their seeds. Toss the seeds as evenly as you can and then rake them shallowly into

If you are planting seeds in rows, make a straight furrow by dragging the corner of a hoe along the row.

Positive Images, Margaret Hensel

Wide-row plantings should be kept thinned so that plants just touch their neighbors. Floating row covers (top, left) protect plants against insect damage and cold weather.

the soil. Broadcast plantings usually need a great deal of thinning, but the closely spaced plants they give rise to shade out weeds and retard water evaporation from the soil.

What is seed innoculant, and how should I use it?

Many gardeners coat seeds of the legume family (beans and peas) with innoculant before planting. Innoculant is a powder that encourages increased numbers of nitrogen-fixing bacteria around the plant roots. Just before planting, moisten the seeds with water, sprinkle the innoculant powder over them in the amount called for on the package, and mix well. Store unused innoculant in the refrigerator, and discard it after the date on the package. Be sure to buy an innoculant powder that is specified for the legume you are planting.

Is there any harm in planting seeds closer together than package advice?

Many gardeners deliberately space plants very close together because they plan to eat the thinnings as their first harvest of the season. Beets, lettuce, radishes (leaves and all), and chard all taste wonderful in the immature stage. Just don't let your vegetables crowd each other as they mature, or your crops will be small and malformed. Another advantage to planting closely is that all those extra seedlings will compete with weeds. Furthermore, a tight row of vegetables with very tender sprouts, such as carrots, seems to have an easier time breaking through heavy soil than do solitary, well-spaced seedlings.

Should I water at seeding time?

If there has not been rain for some time and the soil is dry, water deeply and slowly two days *before* planting. This will give the water time to seep down into the subsoil, yet the topsoil will have time to dry enough so that it won't be muddy when you plant. It's important to get water into the lower layers of the soil, because although you can water the topsoil right after you plant the seeds if you use a fine spray of water so as not to disturb the seeds, it's much harder to get water to the subsoil after seeding. If you water *after* seeding, clay soils can compact and form a crust difficult for new sprouts to push through.

How often should I water after seeding?

Water just as often as it takes to keep the soil moist—in some areas of the country this may be several times daily. Do not let heavy soils crust over from lack of water, or plants may never sprout.

I hate to uproot a healthy little plant. Is thinning really necessary?

It certainly is. Although most plants seem to benefit from being sown rather closely together, once they come up they should not have to compete for root space, water, and sunlight. For recommended final spacing, refer to the seed packet or to our advice for specific varieties in Chapter 6.

Should I thin to the proper spacing all at once or in stages?

In stages is best, if you have the time to return to the garden two or three times as the plants grow larger. Let them stand far enough apart so that their leaves are just touching. The shade these leaves cast will keep the soil from drying out quickly, and will also shade out competing weeds.

Do the plants need to be spaced evenly after thinning?

Don't worry about perfect spacing. While a certain degree of regularity is more apt to result in plants of consistent size, the plants seem to make up for uneven spacing as they grow. Root crops such as carrots and beets will push each other to the side as they grow, so that two perfectly shaped, large roots can grow right next to each other if there is adequate space on their free sides.

CARING FOR YOUR GROWING PLANTS

Controlling Weeds

I've sometimes thought I would never plant vegetables again because weeds give me so many problems. Do I always have to fight a losing battle against weeds?

By developing a weed control program of *prevention*, you can be a gardener of vegetables and not weeds. Remember this cardinal rule: get them while they're young. Plan to put in most of your weeding time in the spring, and after that you probably won't need to weed more than once every two weeks. Avoid introducing into your garden anything—especially uncomposted manure—that may contain weed seeds. Buy weed-free manure, or thoroughly compost fresh manure in a well-heated compost heap. In the fall, plant a cover crop that you can turn under in the spring. Annual ryegrass will crowd out many weeds, and once turned under (before it forms seeds) it will not become a weed problem itself (see page 61). Apply a mulch (see pages 77-78).

What is the best way to weed?

Hand-pulling is effective in most cases, and must be used for established perennial weeds. Large gardens should be cultivated by hoeing or tilling. Early in the season, cultivate 3 inches deep around newly sprouted or transplanted vegetable plants and then apply a mulch. Cultivate more shallowly among mature plants to avoid disturbing roots near the surface. Compost the weeds to conserve their valuable nutrients and bulky fiber.

What about controlling weeds with herbicides?

For home vegetable gardening, avoid chemical herbicides. The risk of damaging your plants is too great and some herbicides will ruin the soil for vegetable culture for several seasons. They may also eventually prove to be dangerous to your own health as well as to the health of the ecosystem.

I have a terrible problem with Bermuda grass. No matter how much I pull, it seems to increase its domain over my garden. What should I do?

The best way is to start a year before you plant a garden in that spot. Till the garden in the summer and seed buckwheat at a rate of 6 ounces per 100 square feet. As soon as it starts to blossom, turn it under and plant another crop of buckwheat at the same rate. Again turn it under when it begins to flower. If the Bermuda grass is still around after that, it will be very weak, and you may be able to pull it all out. If you want to be extra safe, plant one more cover crop, such as winter rye. (Ask your local Extension Service agent to recommend a winter cover crop that does well in your area.) By spring you should have a garden with

A cover crop of winter rye can be planted even on small beds to control weeds and improve the nutrient content of the soil.

Positive Images, Jerry Howard

very few weeds. Buckwheat has a tremendous ability to crowd out troublesome weeds, so this method works not only for Bermuda grass, but for other perennial weeds and rapidly spreading grasses as well. It also vastly improves the texture and nutrient content of a soil.

How can I keep out the perennial weeds and grasses surrounding my garden?

Maintain a swath of bare ground around the perimeter of your garden by turning the soil under with a power tiller; plant a vigorous cover crop such as vetch or clover around the garden; or sink a plastic or metal weed barrier 4 to 6 inches into the ground as an edging.

Are there any crops that don't need much weeding?

Crops that grow tall quickly, such as corn and pole beans, and crops that grow large leaves, such as squash, require less weeding than others because they shade out weeds before they have a chance to take over.

What crops require the most weeding?

Lettuce, carrots, and onions cannot compete with weeds, and need more attention from you and your hoe than most vegetables. In general, the more slowly a crop grows and the less shade it casts, the more weeding you will have to do to grow it.

Mulching

What are the advantages of mulching?

Mulches hold water in the soil, keep down weeds, add bulky organic matter and nutrients to the soil, and keep the soil cool.

What are the best mulching materials?

Among organic materials, dried leaves, buckwheat hulls, ground corn cobs, peat moss, shredded sugarcane (called bagasse and sold as chicken litter), salt-meadow or marsh hay, grass clippings, sawdust, cocoa hulls, wood chips, bark, and straw. Plastic sheeting, usually black, is also popular.

Why do so many gardeners use straw or hay for mulch?

Probably because it is cheap and plentiful. You can buy large bales of it for a few dollars—cheaper if you can find a farmer with spoiled hay he wants to get rid of (hay is not technically straw, but it works well if you apply it thickly). Weed-free organic mulches are usually more desirable, but if you mulch straw deeply enough—up to 1 foot when the plants are reaching maturity—the weeds won't get the sunlight they need to germinate and grow.

How should I go about mulching with hay?

Cut the wire or string from a bale of hay and separate 2- to 3-inch thick pieces from it. Lay these on the soil wherever you don't want anything to grow. This is best done in late spring, or whenever the ground has thoroughly warmed up. If you cover low-growing weeds completely this way, you won't have to bother pulling them up, unless they are right next to your vegetable plants. If your plants aren't sprouted yet, mark the planting locations and lay the mulch around but not over them.

Are plastic mulches good to use?

Plastic mulches, available at nearly all garden centers, are easy to use. You must use black or some other weed-preventing plastic if you want to arrest weeds. Simply roll it out, anchor it with dirt, rocks, wire, or pegs, and poke holes where your plants will be. Used in conjunction with drip emitters, plastic mulches have the added advantage of saving water. On the negative side, the plastic is unattractive, adds no nutrients to the soil, and is at present not a recyclable substance.

Watering

What is the most effective way to save water?

Build good soil that is full of humus.

At what time of day should I water?

Early morning watering is best, although evening watering is good too, provided there is enough time for leaves to dry before nightfall. Although midday watering is not harmful to plants, it is wasteful, since much water evaporates in the heat and sun.

How can I know when to water?

Observe your plants: If they are wilted in the morning or the ground is dry 2 to 4 inches deep, it is time to water. (A dry top inch will do no harm, and is actually desirable for older plants.) Don't hose down the garden because you see your plantings wilting in the heat of day. By sprinkling instead of deep watering, you will encourage plants to develop weak, surface root systems that need constant watering. These plants will suffer badly should even one of these waterings be missed on a hot day. A good rule of thumb is that vegetables should get the equivalent of 1 inch of water each week.

For how long should I water?

Avoid depending on hand watering with the faucet turned up all the way. The top inch or so of soil will get well saturated, but much water will run off the surface to the edges of the beds

instead of deep into the soil where it belongs. It is much better to use a soaker or sprinkler hose, sprinklers, or a drip irrigation system, and to leave the water running slowly for a long time, moistening the soil thoroughly 4 to 6 inches down. After watering, keep the moisture in by laying down as heavy a mulch as possible without smothering plants. If you use a sprinkler, set an empty can in the path of its spray to determine how long it takes for an inch of water to accumulate.

Because deep watering is crucial to a healthy garden, set up a sprinkler in the garden and leave the water running slowly for a long time, so that you are watering to a depth of about 1 inch per week.

Are some garden layouts better than others for conserving water?

Yes. Long, single rows of plants leave much ground exposed, which results in rapid evaporation. Raised beds, advantageous where poor drainage is a problem, hold the plants up higher than ground level and expose them to moisture-robbing wind. Ground-level, closely planted beds offer plants protection from the wind, and offer the soil protection from the sun. Whatever plan you use, mulch your paths, which can act as wicks that draw moisture from the beds and give it up to the sun.

Any other suggestions for saving water?

Put water only where it's needed. Sprinklers that spread water beyond your garden are great water wasters, as are sprinklers that throw water up into the air on windy days. Soaker hose (which is inexpensive), sprinkler hose turned face down, or drip irrigators under mulch put water exactly where it's needed.

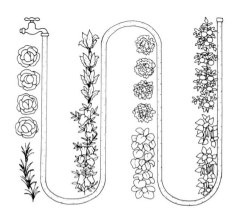

A drip irrigation system such as this, covered with mulch, is an excellent water saver.

79

Is it possible to water too much?

Yes. If the soil becomes soggy, plants don't get enough oxygen and become subject to root rot and other problems.

Are there any crops I should think twice about planting in very dry areas?

The big water-users include corn, cucumbers, lettuce, celery, and leaf and root crops. Tomatoes and peppers, and seed crops, such as beans and sunflowers, can get by with less water. In areas with long growing seasons, plant moisture-loving plants during the months when rainfall will supply your water. Look for drought-tolerant varieties in the seed catalogues.

We live in the high desert of New Mexico, and our water is very alkaline. Will this harm our crops?

Alkaline water creates alkaline soil, which most vegetables do not favor. Dig plenty of compost and organic matter into your soil as often as possible, and plant varieties that tolerate alkaline soils. Consult your Extension Service agent to determine whether you should add sulphur or some other acidifying substance to your soil.

HARVESTING VEGETABLES
_____ • _____

How often should I pick my beans?

Beans, as well as many other crops, such as cucumbers, peas, and summer squashes, should be picked often and continuously. Because its life purpose is to reproduce itself, once one of these plants has produced enough seeds, it will stop producing and die. When you pick continuously, you prevent seeds from maturing, and thus the plant continues to produce. If you can't eat everything you pick, preserve, give away, or sell the excess. Harvest vegetables immediately before cooking them; they will be sweeter, more tender, and more nutritious.

I have heard that it is best, from a nutritional standpoint, to harvest early in the day. Is this so?

In fact, it is usually better to harvest late in the day, when vitamin C content, proteins, and carbohydrates are at their highest points, especially if the sun has been shining hard. On the other hand, crispy crops, such as lettuce and cucumbers, are best picked in the morning. Generally, pick vegetables as close to the time you eat them as possible.

Is it true that beans should not be picked after a rain?

Yes; this promotes the spread of disease. Don't touch your bean plants in the early morning when they are wet with dew or after a rain or a watering.

What is succession planting?

This is a technique whereby a second (or even a third) crop is planted in a bed as soon as possible after a harvest. With good planning, in some areas it may be possible to get three crops by beginning the season with a cool-weather crop, following it with a warm-weather crop, and succeeding that one with another cool-weather crop. Even very small gardens can produce impressively large amounts of food with this method.

How much fertilizer, and of what type, should I add when planting a succession crop?

Use a little less than 1 pound of horse or cow manure per 10 square feet of soil, or a commercial, balanced fertilizer for vegetable crops. In addition, add compost and some bonemeal, as well as a sprinkling of lime if your soil is very acid.

How can I tell whether a succession crop will make it to maturity before the cold weather comes on?

Determine the date of the first fall frost. If there remains sufficient time for the new crop's days to maturity, as indicated on the seed packet, you are on safe ground.

Can a succession crop be planted in the same bed as an established one before the older one is harvested?

That would be risky because you are likely to damage the new crop when you remove the old one. Further, while the old one is still in the ground, it is competing with the new one—probably successfully—for water, light, and nutrients. It is far better to start your second crops in containers and then transplant them, at the seedling stage, after you remove the first crop.

How can I be assured of a continuous supply of lettuce throughout the season?

Succession planting is not confined to following one crop with a different crop. Lettuce and other crops that must be harvested over a short period of time (such as bush beans) will probably give you too big a harvest all at once unless you plant them in stages. Sow such crops at one- to two-week intervals for a continuous harvest of vegetables—and one that you can savor rather than feel overwhelmed by.

Are certain crops best succeeded by certain other ones?

It is best to follow crops such as corn or *Brassicas*, which take a lot of nutrients from the soil (known as "heavy feeders"), with crops such as radishes, which need little fertilizing, or those such as beans or other legumes, which actually contribute rather than remove nutrients. It is especially important not to grow heavy feeders in the same bed year after year.

SUCCESSION PLANTING

VEGETABLES TO CONSIDER FOR SUCCESSION PLANTING

Heavy Feeders

Artichokes
Broccoli
Brussels sprouts
Cabbage
Cauliflower
Celery
Collards
Corn
Cucumbers
Eggplant
Kale
Lettuce
Melons (including watermelon)
Mustard
Okra
Peppers
Parsley
Pumpkins
Rhubarb
Spinach
Squash
Sunflowers
Swiss chard
Tomatoes

Light Feeders

Beans
Beets
Carrots
Chicory
Endive
Leeks
Parsnips
Peas
Potatoes
Radishes
Rutabagas
Shallots
Sweet potatoes
Turnips

Protect tender plants against late spring and early fall frosts by covering them with (A) cut off plastic milk bottles, (B) hot caps, or (C) floating row covers.

Are there any varieties that are particularly good for cold weather growing?

Plant extra-hardy varieties for your fall garden. They will have to be able to germinate in warm weather and produce in cool weather, which is the opposite of the normal cycle for many varieties. Scan the catalogues, and consult your county Extension Service agent for the late-crop varieties best suited to your area.

What can I use to protect plants against fall frosts?

Cloches, mini-greenhouses, and floating row covers will protect against light frosts. With a 1 ½- to 2-foot mulch of straw or dried leaves and snow cover, plants such as kale and other members of the cabbage family, as well as many root vegetables, should survive well into winter. Be sure to mark the location of root vegetables so that you can find them under the snow. In some cases, you may wish to invert bushel baskets over your plants and then cover them with mulch.

FALL CLEANUP

Is there anything I should do to ready the garden for winter after I have taken the last crop of the season from it?

Remove any tough, thick, fibrous plant material, chop it up, and throw it on the compost heap. Turn all remaining crop residue into the soil, spread a layer of manure on the soil, and sow a cover crop of winter rye (see page 61), or apply a 1-foot deep mulch of straw or leaves. If you leave the ground bare through the winter, heavy rains may erode the soil; a cover crop or mulch will add valuable organic matter and nutrients to your soil, improving both its texture and its fertility.

Won't crop residues that are turned into the soil harbor pests and diseases?

No. When you turn them under the soil, they decompose, destroying the pests that were on them, and many kinds of diseases as well. Exceptions are eggplant and tomatoes—burn or dispose of any diseased stems and leaves of these plants.

We live in California, where winter rains bring us our green season in November through April. Should I mulch during the winter, till the ground, and plant a cover crop, or just let the weeds grow?

If weeds grow in abundance in your garden during the winter, you can keep them down either with a thick mulch or a cover crop. Don't let weeds go to seed, or you will have years of constant weeding ahead of you.

Why should I consider container gardening?

People grow vegetables in containers for a variety of reasons: Some have no room for a garden; others are faced with extremely poor soil; some gardeners in the West have a tremendous gopher problem in their in-ground gardens; elderly and handicapped gardeners may choose container gardens for their ease of access; still others grow vegetables in containers because of the highly ornamental nature of many of them. In its most basic form, container gardening requires only a container with sides and a hole in the bottom, soil, seeds, sun, and water. You will find many gardening chores much easier with container gardening: Protective devices against cold snaps or insect pests are simpler to put in place; succession crops are easier to manage by adding or moving containers around; plants are likely to be closer at

CONTAINER VEGETABLE GARDENING

For would-be gardeners with no in-ground space, robust, colorful vegetables can be grown in containers.

Positive Images, Jerry Howard

hand for tending and harvesting, as well as enjoying visually; and, of course, their relatively small size makes them less time-consuming.

How large a container do I need for growing vegetables?

The larger and, especially, the deeper the container the better; plants like plenty of root space. Make 8 inches your minimum, but try to find containers 1 to 2 feet deep.

What sort of container is best?

Plastic is fine, as long as there is a hole or holes in the bottom for drainage. The only material that is not suitable for container-grown vegetables is wood that has been chemically treated to prevent rot.

What kind of soils should I use for container-grown vegetables?

Any one of the following: premixed potting soil, available from garden centers (specify that you will be using it for vegetables); a homemade mixture of equal proportions of compost, coarse sand, and garden loam (light, rich soil, not heavy clay or poor, infertile soil); well-aged compost of neutral to slightly acid pH; a mixture of 1 part peat moss to 1 part sharp sand to 2 parts garden loan, plus fertilizer. Add perlite or vermiculite to your potting mixture if you think it needs extra water- and air-holding capacity.

How often do container-grown plants need to be watered?

Quite often, especially if they receive full sunlight. There is no deep water reserve for container plants, and the combined evaporation of water from the soil and dehydration of leaves and stems from the wind and sun tax the plants' strength. Water at least once a day during hot weather, and check the plants every day whether you water or not. Poke your finger down into the soil an inch or two (1 inch only for very young or small plants); if you feel no moisture down there, it's time to water. When in doubt, water. You will know you've applied enough water when it starts running out of the drain holes. The bigger the pot, the less often you will need to water. Pots with porous sides need more frequent watering. Set containers in water-catching saucers to conserve water.

How should I fertilize container-grown plants? And what kind of fertilizer should I use?

Since container-grown plants need more frequent watering than in-ground plants, the nutrients they need tend to get washed out of the soil. It's best, therefore, to apply a complete fertilizer (such as 5-10-5, depending on the crop) every fifteen to twenty days. Liquid fertilizers, such as fish emulsion, seem to

---

WAYS TO CONSERVE WATER WHEN CONTAINER GARDENING

- Plant in containers with non-porous sides; less water will be lost by evaporation.
- Apply mulch.
- Arrange your container-grown plants close to each other. They will shade each other's soil, create a humid microclimate, offer each other wind protection, and cut down on the amount of reflected heat from the cement, asphalt, or ground they are standing on.
- Set the containers out of the wind.
- Unless they need the extra heat, set container-grown plants away from walls that reflect the sun.
- Root and leaf crops will grow with as little as 4 to 6 hours of direct sunlight a day. Shaded plants use much less water than plants in full sunlight.

work especially well for container-grown vegetables. If you use a granulated fertilizer, make sure it is suitable for vegetables, and water heavily immediately after applying it. Time-release fertilizers are also available at garden centers and through catalogues. Apply all fertilizers according to package instructions, but use less fertilizer than recommended on a more frequent schedule than recommended.

Are there any vegetables that can't be grown in containers?

Asparagus, corn, summer and winter squashes, and melons are not commonly grown in containers, yet all but asparagus among these vegetables have been grown successfully in containers by determined patio gardeners.

What is vertical gardening?

This is a way of arranging low-growing, shade-tolerant plants beneath tall or vining plants. For example, try growing pole beans in containers along a fence or trellis they can climb, with carrots planted in the same containers beneath them. Or let peas climb a net or string trellis placed against a fence or a wall, and sow radishes in the same containers with the peas. The radishes will be ready to harvest before the peas make enough headway to shade them out.

Can I use a container more than once without changing the soil?

Yes, if you improve the soil each year in the same way that you would build soil in the garden (see pages 60-67). Rotate crops of the same plant family from container to container on a four-year schedule to minimize the danger of soil-borne diseases.

Is it all right to move containers once the plants are growing in them?

This is an advantage of container growing: You can move your garden to suit both its needs and your preferences. Set larger tubs and pots on platforms with casters so that they will be easy to move.

Is it possible to have a pest- and disease-free garden?

Like the completely weed-free garden, the completely insect- and disease-free garden is an ideal seldom attained. Your best approach is preventive gardening: Build a healthy soil so that the healthy plants growing in it will be more resistant to disease and insect attack. Plant disease-resistant varieties, give your plants good care (weeding, thinning, and watering), and learn to recognize signs that they are in need of moisture or fertilizer. If insect or disease problems do arise, be prepared to deal with them as soon as possible.

INSECT PESTS AND DISEASES OF VEGETABLES

Insect Pests and Their Controls

INSECT	TYPE OF DAMAGE	CROPS AFFECTED	CONTROL
Aphids	Suck sap from buds, leaves, and stems	Beans, celery, okra, peas, peppers, potatoes	Apply a strong spray of water. Spray with soap and water solution (1 teaspoon mild dishwashing soap to 1 quart water), followed by thorough rinsing later that day. Dust wet plants with wood ashes or diatomaceous earth. Sprinkle bonemeal around plants. Plantings of tansy or pennyroyal may discourage ants.
Asparagus beetles	Eat tips and foliage	Asparagus	Do a thorough fall clean-up (but don't remove dead ferns until spring in cold-winter areas). Use pyrethrum or rotenone to kill larval stage. Shake beetles from plants into a can of soapy water.
Cabbage loopers and cabbage worms	Leaves chewed, sometimes to the extent that plants starve and die	All *Brassicas*, potatoes, radishes	*Bacillus thuringiensis* (Bt). Garden clean-up. Rotation of *Brassicas* and root crops with other plant families on a three-year schedule. Wood ashes spread on soil after each rain or watering.
Cabbage root maggots		*Brassicas*, parsnips, radishes, turnips	Apply lime or wood ashes to soil.
Colorado potato beetles	Defoliation	Nightshade family (potatoes, tomatoes, peppers, eggplants)	Daily hand-pick both adults and eggs, which hide on the undersides of leaves. Rotate Nightshade crops with other plant families. Alternate rows of potatoes and bush beans. Time planting to avoid these, if possible. Turn over the soil in late fall.
Corn borers	Feed inside stalks	Corn	Dust once a week with rotenone or other approved insecticide. Cut a slit in the stalks of infested corn plants and remove worm. Turn under or burn infested stalks in the fall.
Corn earworms	Feed on foliage and kernels. Opens plants to disease and other insect pests	Corn	Just after silk has browned, apply 10 to 20 drops of mineral oil containing rotenone with an eyedropper to the silk tassles or spray mineral oil on tassles. Apply *Bacillus thuringiensis* (Bt) formulated for this purpose. Grow varieties with close-tipped husks. In the fall, turn old broken cornstalks under and thoroughly cultivate soil.
Cutworms	Plants cut off at ground level and left	*Brassicas*, peppers, tomatoes	Place cardboard collars around young seedlings.
Flea beetles	Tiny holes in leaves	*Brassicas*, eggplant, radishes	Sprinkle rotenone or wood ashes on the plants. Observe clean garden practices. Rotate plant families.
Harlequin bugs	Kill young plants by sucking out juices	Cabbage	Rotenone or pyrethrum kills the nymph stage.
Japanese beetles	Chew holes in leaves	Beans	Pheromone traps. Attract birds, which will eat Japanese beetles. Hand-pick small infestations.
Leaf hoppers	Suck plant juices, and in the process introduce disease	Beans, lettuce, Nightshade family	Drape or suspend cheesecloth over plants. Apply pyrethrum or rotenone.
Leaf miners	Wavy, silverish lines through leaves	Beets, spinach, Swiss chard	Pull off all affected leaves and burn them. Drape plants with cheesecloth.

aphid

cutworm

flea beetle

harlequin bug

leafhopper

Insect Pests and Their Controls

INSECT	TYPE OF DAMAGE	CROPS AFFECTED	CONTROL
Mexican bean beetles	Feed on foliage, leaving only leaf skeleton	Beans	Apply rotenone. Set out pheromone traps. Hand-pick. Release predatory worms. Clean up spent bean plants after harvest.
Onion maggots	Tunnel into onion bulbs	Onions	Pull up and destroy plants with infested, softened bulbs. Spread onions throughout the garden rather than in one bed.
Rust fly	Maggot stage feeds on root system	Carrots	Sprinkle wood ashes around the base of plants.
Slugs and snails	Eat entire young plants or leave gaping holes in more mature plants; leave silver trails along ground.	Globe artichokes, lettuce, peppers	After dark, use a flashlight to find slugs. Hand-pick them, and put them in soapy water (wear cotton gloves to avoid getting sticky excretion on your fingers). Trap them under boards and then destroy them. Circle beds with a band of thin copper or a gritty material such as sand, lime, or wood ashes. Trap them in small saucers filled with beer sunk into the ground.
Squash bugs	Cause leaves to wilt and vines to blacken	Squashes	Remove leaves with eggs on them and burn them. Hand-pick. Maintain a clean, neat garden. Throw away old vines after harvest. Rotenone will kill nymph stage. Trap bugs at night by laying a shingle on the ground near plants; overturn shingle and destroy bugs in the morning. Dust with a mixture of wood ashes and slaked lime.
Squash vine borers	Holes in stems; wilted leaves	Cantaloupe, cucumber, squash	Cut borers out of stems. Use rotenone at larval stage. Clean up vines right after harvest. Till soil after harvest to expose cocoons to foraging birds and the elements.
Striped and spotted cucumber beetles	Spread garden disease, such as verticillium wilt	Beans, corn, cucumbers, melons, squash	Use floating row covers over plants to prevent new eggs from being laid. Clean up the garden well after harvest. Mulch with a dry material such as straw. Cultivate in spring and fall to help break the insect's life cycle. Dust with wood ashes, rock phosphate, rotenone, or pyrethrum. Grow plants on trellises.
Thrips	Dark specks on foliage, followed by large, white blotches; drooping shoots; suck plant juices	Onions	Weeds attract thrips. Burn onion tops after harvest. Insecticidal soap or rotenone. Rotate crops.
Tomato horn worms	Defoliation	Tomatoes	Hand-pick. Use *Bacillus thuringiensis* (Bt). (Small white sacks attached to worms are the cocoons of a parasitic wasp that effectively destroys horn worms: Do not kill worms that carry these sacks.)
Weevils	Long snout punctures leaves, stems, and fruits	Peppers, sweet potatoes	Time planting to avoid infestation, if possible. Hill up soil around stems of sweet potato vines. On peppers, hand-pick or control with rotenone. Rotate crops.
Wireworms	Feed on roots and underground stems	Beets, carrots	Choose a new location next year. Avoid planting in places that have recently been converted from sod.

Mexican bean beetle

slug

onion maggot

squash bug

striped cucumber beetle

wireworm

thrip

When seed catalogues offer several different varieties, each of which is resistant to a different disease, how can I know which one would be best for me to grow?

Your Extension Service agent will advise you on which diseases are likely to be common in your area. You can then choose the seed variety that is resistant to those diseases.

What vegetables are most susceptible to disease?

This depends on where you live. In general, cabbage crops, melons, tomatoes, and cucumbers are more susceptible to disease than most others.

I know that farmers rotate their crops. Is this something I should do to combat pests and disease?

By all means. If you keep a garden journal (see page 57) you'll be able to see what you planted where last year, and the year before that. Try not to grow the same kind of crop in the same bed more than once every three years. In fact, avoid growing successive crops from the same plant families: tomatoes, peppers, eggplants, and potatoes belong to the Nightshade family; broccoli, cabbages, kale, collards, and Brussels sprouts are all *Brassicas*; beans and peas are legumes. The time-honored practice of rotating crops not only breaks the life cycles of insects and diseases that feed or live on particular plants, but helps prevent depletion of soil nutrients by such heavy feeders as corn and cabbages.

Insect Pests

What are botanical poisons?

They are plant-derived substances that are poisonous to insects and have little residual effect. They include rotenone, pyrethrum, nicotine solutions, and ryania. Though they are less dangerous than synthetic compounds, they should still be used with caution and a good knowledge of their effects. Like synthetic compounds, botanical poisons are toxic, and may be harmful to beneficial insects as well as insect pests. Rotenone, for example, although harmless to warm-blooded animals, kills bees, which are crucial for plant pollination; to minimize this risk, apply rotenone in the evening when bees aren't flying.

How are botanical poisons applied?

Rotenone and pyrethrum are both applied as a dust or a wetted powder. If they are washed away by rain or overhead watering, they must be reapplied. Pyrethrum, which is made from pyrethrum flowers, must be freshly ground before use. Because it sometimes stuns insects rather than killing them, the insects must be collected and destroyed before they wake up.

Ron West

The cabbage looper moves about with a characteristic looping motion, similar to an inchworm.

Ron West

The Colorado potato beetle is the major pest of potato foliage east of the Rocky Mountains.

Some people are very allergic to pyrethrum, so it should be used with caution. Ryania, effective against aphids, corn borers, Japanese beetles, and codling moths, comes from a Carribean shrub. Like rotenone and pyrethrum, it must be applied frequently.

What are the advantages and disadvantages of commercial insecticides and disease controls?

If you closely follow the label instructions, commercial products work quickly and easily. The products available to home gardeners have been thoroughly tested for effectiveness, and if you are using the right one for the problem you have, they will probably rid your garden temporarily of that insect. Once you start using these chemicals, however, your garden can become dependent upon them because they kill beneficial as well as harmful insects. In addition, used on vegetable gardens, commercial chemicals introduce into your food substances whose long-term effects may not be known. If you do use commercial garden chemicals, carefully follow the label instructions, paying particular attention to the advice on how close to harvest you can safely apply the product.

Helpful Insects and Animals

What are beneficial insects?

A great number of insects further your gardening efforts by feeding on harmful insects. Some of the most common are praying mantises, ladybugs, and lacewing flies (aphid lions). Both ladybugs and lacewing flies prey on aphids. Lacewing flies construct funnel-shaped pits in which to trap aphids, which they then snatch with their long, curved jaws. You may be able to obtain any of these insects from mail-order seed companies or garden centers.

Ladybug.

How can I encourage beneficial insects to live in my garden?

The key is not to *dis*courage them. If you spray to get rid of insect pests, you will unfortunately kill beneficial ones as well. Grow flowering plants among the vegetables to provide pollen and nectar for adult beneficial insects. Dill is very attractive to beneficial worms.

Besides beneficial insects, are there other living things that could help my garden?

Two of the very best are earthworms and birds. Earthworms loosen and aerate the soil, fertilize it with their castings, and help create humus. Yet strong commercial fertilizers, insecticides, and herbicides can kill earthworms. Find out which birds in your area can be most helpful in controlling insect pests, and invite

Beneficial insects, such as this praying mantis, feed on harmful insects in the garden.

them into your yard by providing the kind of houses or trees and shrubbery that they nest in, and providing water and, if necessary, food.

Won't these beneficial birds also eat seedlings in my garden?

Some of them will—if you let them. Protect seedlings with wire enclosures. Narrow lengths of chicken wire folded into long tents work wonderfully on long rows (be sure to enclose the ends of these tents). For wide beds, arch chicken wire over from side to side. Or you can construct movable boxes with scrap wood. Covered with plastic, these can double as mini-greenhouses during early spring.

Are there any other non-chemical controls for areas with great numbers of insect pests?

Cover your seedbeds with floating row covers, available in garden centers or by mail, until plants are fully established.

Plant Diseases

How will I know which diseases my garden might be susceptible to?

Regional seed catalogues usually specify which varieties resist the diseases that most commonly attack in a given area. If you know which diseases you are likely to encounter in your region, you can make wise purchases from any good seed catalogue. For disease problems common to specific plant species, see Chapter 6.

What are the best ways to keep my plants from contracting diseases?

Plant resistant varieties; rotate crops; keep garden free of rotting plant material; promptly discard or burn diseased plants; provide good ventilation around plants; and build healthy soil on an ongoing basis.

Are plant diseases a big problem in home gardens?

They are not usually as much of a problem as for farmers growing large crops of a single kind. A home garden is more varied, with a greater number of checks and balances to control an outbreak of disease or an insect infestation.

Can humans spread disease from plant to plant in a garden?

Yes, this can happen with some vegetables. For example, if you cultivate beans while the leaves are wet, you may spread disease. Or if you smoke cigarettes near members of the Nightshade family, the plants may contract tobacco mosaic.

6 *Favorite Vegetables to Grow*

Artichoke, Globe *(Cynara)*

Where are artichokes best grown?

This perennial vegetable is grown as a winter crop in California, between San Francisco and Los Angeles along the coast, where it gets the mild winters and cool, moist summers in which it thrives. It also finds favorable weather conditions on the Gulf Coast, and in the South Atlantic states. In the eastern states (as far north as Massachusetts), artichokes are a summer crop; and their root crowns are mulched during the winter or dug up and brought indoors.

How can I get artichokes started?

It is best to purchase root divisions. Plant them 6 inches deep, spaced 6 feet apart, as soon as the ground warms in the spring. Alternatively, you can start seeds indoors, planting them ½ inch deep in containers four to six weeks before the last spring frost. Set the seedlings out after all danger of frost is past.

What kind of soil do artichokes need?

Dig plenty of rotted manure or compost into the soil before planting, and give plants a sidedressing of nitrogen halfway through the season. Artichokes need rich, well-drained soil. Mulch with organic materials. If you live in a place that gets hot summer sun, provide your artichokes with partial shade and frequent watering.

◀ *Ruby cabbage and vinca co-exist in serendipitous color harmony.*

Maggie Oster

Globe artichoke: Harvest these intricately formed vegetables when the buds are still firm and tightly compacted.

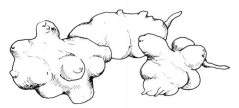

Jerusalem artichoke tuber.

How should I harvest artichokes?

Cut buds off while they are still firm and tightly compacted. The younger the bud, the tenderer the leaves—but the smaller the heart.

Artichoke, Jerusalem *(Helianthus)*

Are Jerusalem artichokes perennial also?

They are, and the name of one popular variety—Stampede— gives you an idea of what these plants will do in your garden if you don't take measures to keep them from spreading.

How should I plant Jerusalem artichokes?

As soon as you can work in the ground in the spring, take small pieces of the tubers with eyes and plant them about 6 inches deep and 18 inches apart. You'll get a big harvest from just a few plants, so unless you have an enormous appetite for them, it is best to plant just a few.

Are Jerusalem artichokes fussy in their needs?

Not at all. You needn't bother with fertilizer, and watering is necessary only in very dry areas. They are troubled by few diseases or pests, except perhaps gophers.

When should I harvest Jerusalem artichokes?

Dig up the tubers in autumn after the tops have died, and store them in plastic bags in the refrigerator until you use them. You can also leave tubers in the ground to harvest as you need them. If you do this in a cold-winter climate, mulch the ground enough to keep them from freezing.

Where can I get planting stock?

You can cut up and plant the Jerusalem artichokes sold in the grocery store as a vegetable. Many seed catalogues sell them, too.

Arugula; Roquette *(Eruca)*

Would you please describe the taste and origins of arugula?

Peppery arugula belongs to the mustard family and adds a nice zip to a tossed salad. Arugula is a long-time standard in Italy and is now popular in nouvelle cuisine.

Can I grow arugula in my garden in New Hampshire?

It should do quite well there, for it prefers chilly, wet weather and cold soil. Early spring, late summer, and fall are best for growing arugula, though in more southern areas where temperatures don't fall below freezing, you can grow it during the winter in a cold frame. It is seldom bothered by either pests or disease.

What are arugula's growing requirements?

Sow a small planting every week or two for a continuous crop; arugula is a very fast-growing and fast-bolting crop. Scatter the seeds across a wide bed and sift ¼ inch of light soil over them. Fertile, well-drained soil is ideal.

What is the best way to harvest arugula?

Pick the leaves off as you need them, or cut the entire plant off a few inches above its base and it will come back again. The plants come to full maturity in forty days, but you can eat thinnings and young tender leaves well before that.

Asparagus *(Asparagus)*

Where will asparagus grow?

Perennial asparagus takes well to all areas of the U.S. except the very coldest North, the Deep South, and Southern California. It actually needs cold winters, and will withstand winter temperatures of -40° F. A well-tended bed will last at least twenty years.

How should I go about starting an asparagus bed?

Prepare a planting bed in late fall or as early in the spring as the ground can be worked. Spread lime if your soil is acid, then dig lots of compost and well-rotted manure 2 feet into the ground. In early spring spade an 8- to 10-inch deep trench in this bed and set in the root crowns, 12 inches apart. Gradually fill in the trench once the plants are actively growing, taking care not to cover the growing tips.

How must I care for my asparagus bed?

Mulch with an organic material, such as compost, that will feed the soil and keep the weeds down. If you don't mulch, weed regularly. If you have acidic soil, spread lime generously on either side of the bed a few days before fertilizing in the spring. Fertilize again after the harvest period. If you live in a cold-winter area, mulch thickly before winter sets in, but pull the mulch aside in early spring so the ground can warm up faster.

I've heard there is a limit to how much asparagus you should harvest. Is this so?

Don't harvest any spears the first year of growth from root crowns (or the first two years of growth from seed). Harvest

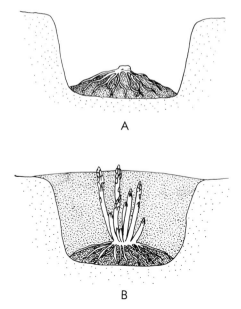

A

B

(A) Set asparagus root crowns in a prepared 8- to 10-inch deep trench, and (B) gradually fill in the trench once the plants are actively growing, taking care not to cover the growing tips.

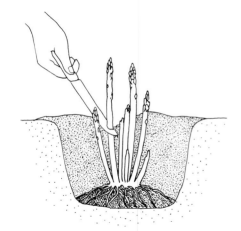

Harvest asparagus by cutting the spear just below ground level when it is about a finger's thickness.

Scarlet runner beans: Often grown as ornamentals, these beans may be used as snap beans or shelled for use in casseroles, soups, or salads.

Positive Images, Margaret Hensel

lightly from root-crown plantings the second spring. If the spears are skinny, don't harvest them at all. Start picking in earnest the third year, and never miss that spring fertilizing. Cut the spears just below ground level when they are about a finger's thickness, and leave enough skinny ones to grow into ferns that will nourish the plant. Don't harvest at all after midsummer.

What are some good rust-resistant varieties of asparagus?

If asparagus rust is a problem in your area, plant Mary Washington or Waltham Washington.

How can I grow white asparagus?

Blanch emerging spears by covering them with airy heaps of a light, organic mulch.

Beans, bush and pole (Legumes)

Which is better to plant—pole beans or bush beans?

Bush beans bear earlier, but over a shorter season. Pole beans produce more abundantly, over a greater length of time (if they are picked regularly), and they have a fuller flavor. Most bean varieties available today are stringless.

Are beans difficult to grow?

Beans grow well in any garden soil. Plant bean seed directly in the ground after all danger of frost is past, two or three weeks after the date of the average last killing frost. The seeds need a soil temperature of at least 60° F. to germinate. Sow bush types 1 inch deep and 2 inches apart, and plant in succession (see page 81) until 50 to 60 days before the first fall frost. Leave 2 or 3 feet of space between rows so you will have room to pick. Wide beds can be planted intensively (see page 58). Beans tend to thin themselves, so plant them close together and let the leaves shade out weeds. Sow pole beans 1 inch deep and 3 inches apart, with 7 seeds around the base of each pole and with 4 feet between rows.

Should beans be fertilized?

If you use commercial fertilizer, apply 2 ½ pounds of a 5-10-10 formula per 100 square feet of row or wide bed. If they are pale, or seem to be growing poorly, apply a sidedressing 3 inches from the plants once they've leafed out and are growing strongly. Beans usually do quite well without very much fertilizer.

Should I water bean plants?

Water them infrequently but deeply, and water at the base of the plants rather than on the leaves, to prevent disease from spreading.

How can I prevent downy mildew or other disease?

Avoid going into your bean patch in the early morning dew, after a rainfall, or at any time when the leaves are wet. Rotate your bean crops.

I've heard that beans are good vegetables to plant in rotation with other crops. Why is this?

Beans are the perfect crop to plant following a crop of heavy feeders, such as corn, because beans take nitrogen from the air and fix it into the soil.

Selected Beans

COMMON NAME	BOTANICAL NAME	EDIBLE FORM	USES	DESCRIPTION	GROWING INFORMATION
Azuki (or Adzuki)	*Vigna angularis*	Immature pods, shelled, or dried	In Japan, dried azuki beans are used for desserts as well as in hearty vegetable stews	Small, brick-colored beans; bushy, delicate plant	Best started indoors in peat pots, as they take 120 days to mature
Chickpeas; garbanzos	*Cicer arietinum*	Dried	Use in Middle Eastern dishes, salads, and soups	Lacey, unusual plants; one or two peas to a pod	Require over 100 days to mature, and prefer a warm, dry climate
Fava; broad; horse	*Vicia faba*	Immature pods (2 to 3 inches long) or shelled	Eat young beans like snap beans (some people of Mediterranean descent are allergic to fava beans)	Large, shiny, plump pods, each with five to seven fat, green beans; sweet-smelling flowers are white with black centers	Semi-hardy—in warm climates, plant them in late fall; in the North and East, plant them in the spring as soon as the soil can be worked
Lima	*Phaseolus limensis*	Fresh	Alone or in casseroles and soups	Both bush and pole varieties; heavy producers	Prefer cool summers (in hot climates grow the more heat-tolerant butterbeans, such as Henderson's Bush)
Mung	*Vigna radiata*	Sprouts	Chinese dishes such as stir-frys and chop suey	Small, green bean	Need a long, hot, preferably humid, summer
Runner	*Phaseolus coccineus*	As snap bean, or shelled	Alone or in casseroles, soups, or salads	Beautiful, profuse red or white flowers; large, shiny, handsome beans; often grown as an ornamental; perennial in warm-weather areas	Same as string beans
Soybeans	*Glycine max*	Shelled or dried	Tofu, soy milk, tempeh, salad oil, cattle feed; boil green soybeans in their pods for 5 minutes, shell them, and then cook for 15 minutes more; use dried beans in casseroles	Round, almost white bean	Drought-tolerant, easy-to-grow; green varieties mature in 75 days; dried beans mature in 105 to 120 days

When should I begin harvesting my beans?

To keep beans producing, start picking them (including their stems) as soon as you see the first edible bean—that is, as soon as their seeds begin to show through their skin, or even earlier if you like them extra tender. If you have more beans than you can harvest and eat, let some plants go completely to seed, and concentrate on harvesting a few plants thoroughly. Shell these "seedy" beans and eat the seeds fresh, as you would limas. If they're not hybrids, dry them and use them as seed next year.

Dried beans are so inexpensive. Are they really worth growing for drying and shelling?

Most drying beans are good to eat at the immature green bean stage and good also shelled and eaten green. This makes them multipurpose plants in every way. Furthermore, there are a good many wonderful drying beans for sale in catalogues that simply can't be purchased in most stores. Many of them, such as Jacob's Cattle, Soldier, Yellow Eye, and Swedish Brown beans, are stunning in their beauty as well as their flavor when you bake or boil them.

When should I pick beans for shelling and eating fresh?

Shelling beans are eaten in the stage between green and dried. If you plant them once a week over the first month of the growing season, you can have fresh shelling beans all season long.

Pole beans readily climb twine provided for them and produce more abundantly and for a longer time than bush beans.

Martha Storey

Ann Reilly

Beets *(Beta)*

Why are beets so popular with vegetable gardeners?

Beets are one of the most versatile vegetables you can grow. They are hardy—you can start them early or late—and if you mulch them well, you can harvest them even after unmulched ground has frozen. Their leaves have an exquisite, sweet, yet mildly acid flavor, and their roots lend themselves well to pickles, soups, and salads, or simply serve boiled beets whole or sliced with butter. Look for cylindrical slicing beets, golden or white salad beets, and varieties developed for leaf flavor.

How should I plant beet seeds?

Spread lime if your soil is acid. Sow beet seeds when the ground has begun to warm up in the spring. Beet seeds come in clusters, so sow thinly, about 10 seeds per foot, ½ inch deep in rows 12 inches apart. You can keep planting every two weeks until midsummer, and again six to eight weeks before the first frost. Don't plant beets during the hot months. Although they will grow in clay soil, beets prefer light, sandy soil and steady moisture. Mulch after sowing.

When should I begin harvesting beets?

Thin beets when the greens and young roots are the size of a quarter, and eat the thinnings. A few leaves may be picked as the beets mature. In warm climates, beets can be left in the ground in the fall, and harvested through the winter as needed.

Beet: Both tops and roots of Burpee's Golden beets are tender and sweet.

Broccoli *(Brassica)*

Should I sow broccoli seeds directly in the ground or buy seedlings?

Broccoli is usually transplanted using purchased seedlings or seedlings begun indoors, rather than directly seeded in the ground. Early plantings should go in during March and April; later plantings, if you have sustained cool weather, can go in during May. For a fall harvest, plant in late summer. Broccoli can take light frosts in the fall.

How should I plant broccoli?

Make sure your soil is rich in nutrients—especially calcium— and well drained. Space transplants 18 to 24 inches apart in rows 2 to 3 feet apart. Plant seeds ½ inch deep, twelve seeds to a foot, and thin to the same spacing as for transplants. These thinnings, if handled carefully, can be used to start another row.

Broccoli: Purple-headed broccoli turns emerald green when cooked.

Do broccoli plants require watering and fertilizing?

Provide continuous soil moisture, but don't flood the roots. Mulching helps. Apply a nitrogen fertilizer as a sidedressing to established plants every month or so to keep them growing fast.

When should broccoli be harvested?

Cut off the heads a few inches down the stem when the flowers have formed but are still tight. If you leave a good amount of stem, side shoots will form, which may be cut and used later. Some varieties are known for producing lots of side shoots over a long period. Don't let any buds go to flower.

Brussels sprouts *(Brassica)*

When can I plant Brussels sprouts?

Brussels sprouts need cool weather. Although they will withstand a certain amount of summer warmth, they won't thrive in hot summers. The cool, damp climate of the central coast of California is ideal for Brussels sprouts. Set out transplants (after broccoli) in mid-May through mid-June for a fall harvest. If you sow seed outdoors (you need a long growing season to do so), plant it the same way as you would broccoli seed.

What kind of soil and fertilizer needs do Brussels sprouts have?

Give them rich, well-drained soil, steady water, and side-dressings of nitrogen-rich fertilizer.

How can I know when to harvest Brussels sprouts?

The sprouts, or buds, mature from the bottom of the stalk up. Remove leaves as they turn yellow; the leaves will usually snap off easily as far up the stem as the sprouts are ready to cut. Twist-snap the sprouts off when they're firm. Very small Brussels sprouts make fine baby vegetables. Leave Brussels sprouts in the garden for the first light frosts, which improve this vegetable's flavor. Before the first hard freeze, cut entire stalks, remove the leaves and the crown, and hang them upside down in a cool, dark, dry place. They'll keep for many weeks this way.

Cabbage *(Brassica)*

Can I grow cabbage in the South?

Cabbage is a cool-weather crop, needing from 60 to 125 days to mature, depending on the variety. In the South, you'll need to plant cabbage in fall to mature in winter. Plant short-season, early cabbage in mid- to late winter, so that it will mature before extreme heat sets in.

How should I prepare for planting cabbage?

See to it in the fall that your cabbage bed is well limed so that it has sufficient calcium content and pH balance. Dig in fresh, uncomposted manure during the fall so that it will decompose sufficiently by spring.

Should I begin seeds indoors or can I plant cabbage directly into the garden?

You can start seeds indoors for transplanting four to six weeks before the last frost. Set the seedlings outdoors after the last frost, spacing them 12 to 18 inches apart in rows 2 to 3 feet apart. Alternatively, you can direct-seed, but wait until the soil is at least 50° F. and then sow four seeds per foot, ½ inch deep, in rows 2 to 3 feet apart. Thin to 12- to 18-inch spacings in the rows. In general, those varieties that take the longest to mature also keep the longest. If you're planting late varieties, which mature just in time for winter storage, get them started as soon as possible in the spring.

Does cabbage require fertilizer and extra watering?

Cabbages are heavy feeders, and should be planted in well-fertilized, rich soil. Fertilize a week before planting, and in addition, apply one or two sidedressings of fertilizer during the growing season. Since cabbage roots are shallow, the plants need frequent watering during dry weather. If the heads crack, the cabbages are growing too fast. This can come from too much fertilizer at once, or from a sudden burst of growth when rains fall after a long dry spell. To prevent further cracking, clutch the heads in your hands and give them a half-turn twist. This will break some of the roots and slow the plants' growth.

How should I harvest cabbages?

Pull up the plants, roots and all, when the heads are mature. Cut off the root and compost it after chopping it into pieces with your spade.

What is Chinese cabbage?

This large group of cabbages is divided into two categories: heading and nonheading. The heading types *(Brassica pekinensis)* include the Napas (also called Michili, celery cabbage, and Pe Tsai), which are often found in grocery stores. The most common of the nonheading Chinese types *(Brassica chinensis)* is Bok Choy (also called Pac Choi). Most all Chinese cabbages, and in particular the heading types, require cool growing conditions. Like all cabbages, they should grow fast and steadily for the best flavor and health. You can transplant or direct-seed. An excellent nonheading variety is Mei Qing Choi, also known as Baby Bok Choy.

Cabbage: A cool-weather crop, cabbage needs from 60 to 125 days to mature, depending upon the variety.

Maggie Oster

Carrots *(Daucus)*

When can I begin planting carrots?

Beginning two weeks before the last spring frost, plant carrots in succession (see page 81) throughout the season until sixty days before the first killing frost. Although germination takes longer in cold soils, in mild-winter areas you can sow carrot seed all year round, as long as rains don't wash seeds away before they have time to sprout. Sow seeds ¼ inch deep in rows 1 to 2 feet apart. Give this tiny, shallow-planted seed some special attention, for it germinates slowly (one to three weeks). If you have heavy soil, water it well the day before planting; cover the seed with peat moss after planting. Water with a very fine mist. Sow radish seeds among the carrot seeds, at a ratio of about one radish seed to nine carrot seeds. The radish seeds will take only a few days to germinate, so they'll come up and mark your carrot rows for you while also gently loosening the soil around the carrots to give them a good start. Pull the radishes as soon as they are mature.

I have tried growing carrots, but my soil is heavy and my carrots are always crooked. Any suggestions?

Try growing the short, stubby, or even round varieties that are widely available today. Since these carrots don't extend deeply into the soil, they are less likely to twist or fork, and they are easy to harvest. You can also dig a trench and fill it with lighter soil, or build up a raised bed of lighter soil.

Do carrots need watering and fertilizing?

Keep carrot seeds moist until they sprout, and then water infrequently but deeply, so that the roots will reach down for moisture. Avoid using fresh manure; it causes the roots to be hairy and to fork. Too much nitrogen will produce wonderful foliage but not very good roots. Carrots are not heavy feeders and shouldn't be overfertilized. Weed carrots faithfully.

When can I start harvesting carrots?

Eat baby carrots from your thinnings, usually within forty days of planting. When they reach about finger thickness they will be extremely sweet. Thin carrots to stand 2 inches apart. If your soil gets really hard, soak it well before attempting to pull your carrots. If they break, you'll have to dig them out.

How should I store carrots for the winter?

The best way is to layer them in damp sand or sawdust, but they keep a long time in a ventilated plastic bag or in burlap if you put them in a dark, cool place. Or mulch the ground with hay bales or plastic bags of leaves to keep the ground from freezing, so that you can dig them up through the winter.

Carrots: For the best carrots, weed faithfully and thin so that plants stand 2 inches apart.

Cauliflower *(Brassica)*

Our summers are hot. Is it possible for me to grow cauliflower?

Start cauliflower indoors in the spring eight to ten weeks before the last spring frost or in the late summer, 80 to 100 days before the first killing frost. Cauliflower seedlings can go in the ground in the spring two weeks before the last expected frost.

How big should my seedlings be before I put them in the garden?

Seedlings should be four to five weeks old (and no older) when you set them out. Be sure to harden them off first (see page 71). Space the plants 18 to 24 inches apart in rows 2 to 3 feet apart.

How much water and what kind of soil should I give cauliflower?

The most important thing you can do for your cauliflower is to give it a regular supply of moisture so that it grows fast. Never let the soil dry out, but don't flood it, either. Cauliflower is best when the weather is cool. Sprinkle the plants with water during hot spells to keep them cool, and to maintain a humid atmosphere around them. Cauliflower prefers "sweet" soil—that is, soil with a pH a little on the alkaline side (between 6 and 7).

How can I be assured of white, sweet-tasting heads?

You must blanch the stalks by bending the outer leaves together over the curds (center) and tying them in place once the curds reach about 3 inches in diameter. Leave them this way until the head matures. Make sure the head is dry when you tie it up, and arrange the leaves in such a way that water can't trickle through to the curds and rot them. Untie the leaves of a few plants now and then to see how the heads are forming and whether any water is getting in.

When should I harvest cauliflower?

Cut the heads from the stalks when the curds are still tight, usually one or two weeks after tying them up. If the weather is getting hot, check them often, or they'll get away from you and begin to swell and form flowers.

I've seen self-blanching varieties advertised in many catalogues. What does this mean?

The leaves of these types grow over the curds, saving you the trouble of tying them up. Romanesco cauliflower (sometimes called Romanesco broccoli) has beautiful, pointed, green curds that look like little towers. Purple cauliflower, which turns green when cooked, is also available.

To be assured of white, sweet-tasting cauliflower, blanch stalks by bending the outer leaves together over the curds and tying them in place until the head matures.

Celery *(Apium)*

Isn't celery difficult to grow?

If you have a soil that holds water well, and a three-month cool-weather season, you can grow celery. If you have only two months of weather that is cool but not freezing, you can still give celery a try if you plant it in a spot where you can supply a little shade during hot spells.

How are celery seeds begun indoors?

In the spring, sow seeds in a light potting soil in flats, ten to twelve weeks before the soil warms up. Sow the seeds thinly and very shallowly (about ⅛ inch deep), and keep the soil in the flat warm and moist (up to 75° F.) until the seedlings emerge after two to three weeks. Once they're up you can let the soil get cooler—down to 60° F. When the plants are about 2 inches tall, transplant them into individual containers. Two or three weeks after the last expected frost, set the plants out in the garden, 6 inches apart in rows 2 to 3 feet apart.

In warm-summer areas, sow celery seeds in a well-prepared outdoor seed bed, about thirteen to fifteen weeks before the first expected frost. The plants will withstand light frost but not hard freezing in the fall. To transplant from seed beds into the garden,

A frame of boards and burlap around this row of celery blanches the plants, creating more tender hearts and stalks.

Maggie Oster

dig the seedlings carefully to avoid breaking the fine root system. Avoid doubling up or bunching the roots when you set them in their garden bed; pack the soil firmly around the plants, at the same level as it was in the seed bed.

Do celery plants need to be watered frequently?

Celery requires abundant and very consistent moisture, which means that soils with poor water-holding ability should be improved with plenty of organic matter.

Should I fertilize celery heavily?

Sidedressings of fairly rich fertilizer two or three times during the growing season will keep the plants strong and fast growing. But don't use too much fertilizer. Look closely at the plants as they grow and base your fertilizer applications on what you see rather than on any formula. Phosphorus (see page 64) promotes strong stalks. Make sure that your soil has adequate calcium in it by adding lime (if your soil is acid), gypsum, crushed eggshells, or phosphate rock.

Must celery be blanched?

Blanching creates paler, more tender hearts and stalks. One traditional blanching method involves planting celery in shallow trenches and then filling in the trenches with soil as the plants grow tall. The disadvantage of doing it this way is obvious to anyone who has ever spent a lot of time cleaning dirt from celery hearts and stalks before cooking them. Better methods of blanching are to pile straw around your celery plants, lean boards up against them, or tie shopping bags around the stalks with string—anything that blocks the sun but allows the circulation of air. Make sure plants are dry before you cover them, and leave the tops uncovered.

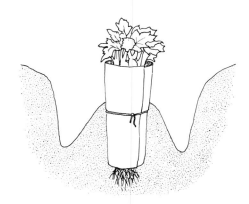

Celery may be blanched by wrapping stalks with paper and piling soil against them.

How should I store celery after harvest?

Pull up the entire plant once the stalks are blanched. To store celery, leave the roots on, spray the stalks and foliage with cool water, and then shake the water off. Let the stalks dry but keep the roots moist. Now plant them again in a shallow trench, in boxes in a cool cellar or in a cold frame, with the temperature just above freezing. You can keep celery fresh for many weeks this way.

Is celery troubled by diseases?

Celery blight is sometimes a problem. Rotate your crops to avoid it. If it occurs, dust or spray with bordeaux mixture every week or ten days, taking special pains to coat the lower leaves, especially the undersides. If very dry weather occurs, the disease may abate and you can stop treatment.

Chicory; Escarole; Radicchio (*Cichorium*)

When should I plant radicchio, or red-headed chicory?

In mild-winter areas, sow seeds in the fall. The plants will mature by spring, and fall frosts will give the plants the lovely red color they are known for. Where winter temperatures drop below 10° F., sow seeds in late May to early June. Cover the seeds with a very thin, ¼-inch layer of soil. Space them rather closely, but thin later to 8 to 12 inches apart. If you are growing a variety that needs cutting back, shear it back to a stub in early September. Within 4 to 6 weeks you'll be harvesting mature plants.

How are escarole and chicory grown?

Treat them like lettuce, and harvest before the first hard frost. Because they mature more slowly than lettuce, allow ninety days from sowing to grow large heads.

Collards (*Brassica*)

I don't know much about collards. Are they a good vegetable to grow?

Collards are non-heading cabbages that have much to recommend them. They are high in calcium, iron, and vitamins A and C. They don't mind frost, but can take considerable summer heat, which is perhaps one of the reasons why they are so widely grown in the South. Collards are also especially delicious after they have been touched by frost in the fall.

When should I plant collards?

Sow seeds in the ground at any time in the growing season, giving them eighty to ninety days to mature. Hot-area plantings are often made in the summer, so that the plants will mature in time to be touched by frost and thereby sweetened. In cold climates, seedlings are set out in the spring. Early spring to mid-spring plantings yield summer crops. Sow twelve seeds to the foot, ¼ to ½ inch deep in rows 2 feet apart. Thin the plants as they grow (and eat the thinnings) until they are growing one plant per foot.

What growing conditions should I provide for collards?

Collards are grown in the same way as other *Brassicas*. Supply calcium in the form of lime (in acid soils), gypsum, crushed eggshells, or phosphate rock for good harvests of nutrient-rich greens. You may need to stake the plants once they get leggy and top-heavy.

How are collards harvested?

Pull or cut off the lower leaves as you need them. Or cut out the tender, central loose head. Their preparation and uses are much like spinach or any other cooking greens.

Corn (*Zea*)

What are the various types of sweet corn?

Standard is the traditional variety. It has a crisp, crunchy texture but once picked, it loses its sweetness. SE (Everlasting Heritage, EV, or Sugar Enhanced) varieties are sweeter and more tender than standard varieties for a longer period after harvest. These varieties may be planted within 25 feet of standard sweet corn without risk of cross-pollination. SH_2 (Supersweet, Extra Sweet, or Xtra Sweet) varieties are very sweet and remain sweet long after harvest, because their sugar turns to sucrose rather than starch as in standard sweet corn. Their seed is shriveled and smaller than other corns. SH_2 varieties must be isolated at least 100 feet (or planted at different times) from both standard and SE varieties or both crops will produce tough, starchy kernels.

When can I plant corn?

The soil at planting time should be at least 70° F. for SE or SH_2 varieties and 65° F. for standard sweet corn. Particularly for SE and SH_2 varieties the soil should stay quite moist until the seedlings appear. As a rule, the newer corn types are not as hardy as standard hybrid varieties, and must be fertilized and watered with extra care.

What can I do to get my first corn extra early?

Plant an early variety such as Early Sunglow or Earlivee in a warm, sunny location. If the soil is still cold, use seed that has been treated with a fungicide; soak it for twenty-four hours in warm water. Plant it a little deep, and don't fertilize at all until the danger of frost is past. Black plastic mulch will help warm the soil, and a polyethylene tunnel placed over the rows will warm the air temperatures around the plants. You can also start corn in flats and transplant it, providing the seedlings are not kept too warm and then set out in cold ground too early. Peat pots or homemade tubes of newspaper work best as starter containers, because you don't disturb the roots when you transplant.

How is corn normally planted?

Sow seeds 1 to 1½ inches deep at 4-inch intervals, thinning the seedlings to 8- to 12-inch spacings. Space corn rows 2 to 3 feet apart so that you don't get scratched when harvesting. Corn needs steady moisture to germinate, so water your corn patch if

When the corn tassles, as shown here, apply a sidedressing of fertilizer and water it in well.

Maggie Oster

the weather is dry. During hot weather, when the soil is already warm, you can mulch a newly planted bed with a thin layer of organic material to keep the soil from drying out in the hot sun.

The row of corn I planted last year never bore for me. What was wrong?

If you planted one long row, chances are it was poorly pollinated. In order to ensure pollination, corn must be planted in blocks of at least four rows. Different varieties should go in different blocks rather than every other row. Don't plant sweet corn near field corn, or the field corn will pollinate your sweet corn and give it tough kernels.

Does corn need much care?

Cultivate your corn bed to kill weeds until the plants reach a foot high. After that, cultivate very shallowly. Hill up dirt against the corn stalks so that you don't have to cultivate too close to them. Better yet, apply a mulch to keep weeds down and retain moisture in the soil. Corn is a very heavy feeder, and should be planted in soil that has been fertilized with a complete, nitrogen-rich fertilizer. Follow this with a sidedressing of high-nitrogen fertilizer when the corn is almost a foot high. When the corn tassles, give yet another sidedressing of fertilizer, along with extra water, and continue to water steadily until the ears ripen.

Should I remove suckers (side shoots) from corn stalks?

No, this old practice has no apparent benefits.

How can I tell whether my corn is ready to harvest?

Corn is ready to harvest when the silks have turned brown and dry. Squeeze the tops of the ears to see if they are filled out. If they seem to be, peel back the husks and have a look. If the kernels are full and round and ooze milk when you poke them with a fingernail, they are ready to pick. Don't peel back any more husks than necessary, for this exposes the ears to insect attack.

Is it true that you should put the water on to boil before you go out to harvest the corn?

To assure the freshest tasting corn with the old standard varieties, the faster you can get it from the garden to the table, the better. The new supersweets have so much sugar that an hour or so wait will cause no discernible loss in sweetness. If you refrigerate them promptly, they will still taste wonderful even a day later.

How can I avoid having the wind blow over stalks?

This problem is called "lodging." Plant resistant varieties, and protect planting with windbreaks. If the stalks fall over, though there has been little wind, look for European corn borer damage.

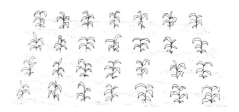

Corn must be planted in blocks of at least four rows to assure good pollination.

A white gall that later turned black appeared on my corn last year. What was it?

It was corn smut, a fungus growth that comes through the stem into the ear or tassle. It is one of the most disturbing-looking corn diseases, but usually causes no serious problems. Cut out these galls, and either burn them or wrap them in plastic and dispose of them—but *not* in your compost heap. Also destroy smutty ears as soon as you find them. Plant a smut-resistant variety next time.

Crows got in and pulled up all my corn seedlings to eat the plump kernels at their bases. How can I keep them away?

The best method to combat birds is to protect newly planted rows with long, narrow tents of 18-inch chicken wire. Be sure to close the tents on either end, or the birds will simply hop inside one end of the tent and eat their way to the other. Some gardeners report success with deep mulches, though these aren't recommended for cold soils.

The worst problem I've had in raising corn is raccoons. Is there any defense against them?

Raccoons seem to be better than people are at calculating the ripeness of corn. 'Coons will climb almost anything but an electrified fence—which they may dig their way under. You could try one of the traps that captures animals without harming them, but if you don't have experience with releasing raccoons from a live trap, seek advice from your local animal shelter or from the trap's manufacturer. Raccoons can be as vicious as they are cute, and they can transmit rabies.

I grew wonderful corn one year, but the next year when I grew it in the same place, my harvest wasn't nearly as good. Was it the weather?

Weather might have had something to do with it, but it is more likely that the soil was exhausted of nutrients. It is best not to grow corn twice in the same place until three or four years pass. Follow heavy-feeding corn crops with heavy-giving crops of peas or beans (see page 81).

My cornstalks grew tall and heavy, but bore no ears. What might the problem have been?

They could have been spaced too close or been given too much nitrogen. This happens, too, if plants are not sown in 4-row blocks.

What causes stalks to tassle when they are only 2 or 3 feet tall?

Stress caused by acid soil, dry weather, dark days, or a lack of fertilizer.

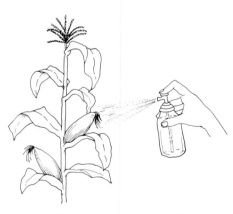

After pollination has taken place, spray mineral oil on browning corn silk to deter corn earworms.

What would cause corn ears to fail to fill out?

It could be nutrient-poor soil, plants that are spaced too closely, cross-pollination with field corn, or corn borers in the stalk just below the ear.

Cucumbers *(Cucumis)*

Where should I plant cucumbers in my garden?

Cucumbers need partial shade and something to climb on. They look delightful growing rampantly on a fence or porch railing, and the fruit will be easier to harvest. Simply plant them under a fence, or against a wall onto which you can hang strings and tie the vines to the strings or fence with strips of cloth where necessary. Plant bush varieties in containers.

Should I start cucumber plants indoors?

Cucumbers are warm-weather plants, and many gardeners thus start them indoors so that they can have seedlings heading skyward in the garden just as soon as the warm weather begins in earnest. Indoors, plant cucumbers in soil that is about 70° F. during the day and 60° F. at night. Start them four weeks before setting them outside. Transplant the seedlings with great care after all danger of frost is past. If the weather is still cool, set them under hot caps. Space them 6 inches apart in rows 4 to 5 feet apart.

What kind of soil do cucumbers need?

Good quality garden loam that is fairly high in nutrients will support cucumbers. The soil should not be acid, and it should be well drained. Keep the ground moist at all times, especially during hot spells, or the fruit will turn bitter.

How should I care for cucumbers?

Weed faithfully until the plants are large enough to shade the ground. Mulch once the soil is warm, not only to keep down weeds and hold moisture in the soil, but also to keep mud from splashing onto the leaves and spreading disease. When the plants are knee high, sidedress them with bloodmeal, cotton-seed or soy meal, or some other nitrogen-rich fertilizer.

How can I get my cucumber plants to keep producing?

Check the plants every day during peak production and harvest often, for once a cucumber plant satisfies itself with a few mature fruits, it stops producing and dies. Young cucumbers taste better than aged ones, so pick them smaller than the ones you see in the store. Avoid touching the plants when they're wet, so that you won't spread disease.

Positive Images, Jerry Howard

Cucumber: Give cucumber vines partial shade and something to climb on.

Eggplant (*Solanum*)

Is it true that eggplant makes a good ornamental plant?

Long grown as an ornamental as well as a food plant, eggplant comes in white, green, yellow, and pink, as well as the familiar purple varieties. Specialty vegetable catalogues carry seed for Thai, Japanese, Chinese, Indian, Persian, Italian, and other varieties.

Should I begin eggplant indoors?

Yes. Start seeds indoors eight to ten weeks before warm weather has arrived for good. The seeds need warm (at least 70° F.) soil in order to germinate. When you transplant them into the garden, space them 18 to 24 inches apart in rows 24 to 36 inches apart. Protect seedlings from cold snaps with hot caps.

What care should I give eggplant?

Sidedress the plants with a balanced fertilizer three weeks after transplanting them, and again when the fruits are just beginning to emerge from the blossoms. Water regularly and deeply. Mulches are valuable once the soil has warmed thoroughly. Stake the plants if they begin to be pulled down by heavy fruits.

How can I tell when eggplant is ready to be harvested?

Harvest the fruits while the skin is still tight, when the flesh gives a little to finger pressure. The seeds should not yet be brown. For an extended harvest, keep picking the plants as the fruits mature.

How can I protect eggplants against verticillium wilt?

Grow eggplants in containers of commercial, sterilized potting soil. Apply a soluble fertilizer to container-grown eggplants once a week.

Last year we had an unusually cool season after I planted my eggplant and all the new blossoms fell off. How could I have helped?

Temperatures below 50° F. or above 90° F. stress eggplant and cause blossoms to drop. Plenty of compost worked into the soil before planting and a thick mulch of organic material will help the plants withstand temperature extremes.

Escarole. See Chicory

Eggplant: An ornamental as well as a food plant, eggplant is available in white, green, yellow, and pink, as well as the familiar purple varieties.

Ann Reilly

Leeks (Allium)

Are leeks complicated to grow?

Although they take a very long time to reach maturity, leeks are a simple and satisfying crop to grow. Their culture takes more attention than skill.

Will leeks reach maturity in my New England garden?

You should be able to grow hardy early varieties such as King Richard and Blue Solaise with fine success.

Should I begin leeks indoors?

If you have a short growing season, it is crucial. Start leeks from seed sown ¼ inch deep in flats, twelve weeks before the last frost. Thin the sprouts so that each plant has 1 inch of space. When the leeks are pencil thick, transplant them into the garden 4 to 6 inches apart in rows 8 to 12 inches apart. In more southern areas with 140 days of growing season, gardeners can start leeks outdoors in mid-January to mid-February, or plant seeds in August through November for harvest the next spring.

How can I blanch leeks?

The traditional way to plant leeks is to set them in 6-inch furrows, and then gradually fill them in to blanch the stalks as the plants grow. This technique has two disadvantages: It requires a lot of work, and it gets grit into the folds of the stalks. To save work in both garden and kitchen, try wrapping the leeks with brown paper, or slipping 6-inch tubes of cardboard or plastic (such as thin-walled, 2-inch, PVC pipe) over the stalks when they're almost an inch thick. Even if you don't get around to blanching your leeks, they will be fine in soup.

When should I harvest leeks?

Leek varieties vary in maturity dates from 70 to 140 days. Harvest your leeks close to their maturity date, if they have reached 1 to 2 inches in diameter. Don't let them send up flower stalks, for they will be too tough to be of value in the kitchen.

Lettuce (Lactuca)

How can I choose among the many lettuce varieties available?

Advances in breeding, coupled with recent importations of English, French, Italian, other European, and Scandinavian varieties, have brought what seems to be a boundless choice of lettuce varieties to today's gardener. Some of the most beautiful

Ann Reilly

Leeks: Blanch leeks as shown here by planting them in 6-inch furrows and gradually filling in the furrows with soil as the plants grow.

Maggie Oster

Lettuce: If you begin lettuce indoors, be sure to harden it off before setting it into the outdoor garden.

are the frilly red and green, and the cream-colored, looseleaf lettuces, such as Lollo Rosa. Pirat is a butterhead type with bronze-mottled leaves known in Switzerland as Sprenkel lettuce. Choose lettuces according to the temperatures you are likely to have at different times of the season. Winter varieties respond to short days. Fall-planted lettuces are especially cold-hardy. Spring- and summer-sown varieties are less likely to become bitter or bolt to seed (mature too rapidly to seed).

How can I be assured of fresh, tender lettuce all season?

Sow small amounts of seed every seven to ten days so that new plants are continually coming along.

Should I start lettuce plants indoors?

Lettuce is a prime candidate for starting indoors in flats or pots and transplanting into the garden as early as the ground can be worked. Harden it off first (see page 71), and water after transplanting. Outdoors, sow seeds ¼ inch deep, and thin so that each plant has 8 inches of space—12 inches for heading and Romaine types. Be sure not to plant seed too deep, because it needs light to germinate.

Can I grow lettuce where summers get quite hot?

In such areas, you'll have best success growing lettuce in the spring and fall. Midsummer plantings in hot areas may work if you can find a partially shaded area or provide shade with a 50-percent shade cloth screen from 10 a.m. to 4 p.m. Bolt-resistant varieties are your best bet, though even they are cool-weather plants (60° to 65° F. is ideal), developed to stand up to hot spells, not continuous hot weather.

Can I start heading lettuce or Romaine directly in the vegetable garden?

These varieties take longer to mature and must thus be started indoors in short-season areas. Unseasonal light frosts won't damage most varieties at the seedling stage.

Does lettuce need to be watered?

A constant supply of water is perhaps the most important requirement of lettuce, especially during weather above 65° F. Otherwise, your plants will produce bitter greens and be more likely to attract pests. Fertilize the ground before planting with compost, manure, or a complete fertilizer, and then moisten it well whenever it is the slightest bit dry.

How is lettuce harvested?

If some lettuces, such as Curly Oakleaf, Salad Bowl, Matchless and other looseleaf types, are cut back to their roots, they will grow another, smaller crop of leaves. This is called "cut-and-come-again" culture, and is best done when the plants are 4 to 6 inches high. The standard way to harvest lettuce is to cut off heading types, including Bibb, just below the head, and to pull leaves a few at a time from looseleaf types.

Melons *(Cucumis)*

Are melons related to cucumbers?

Two kinds of common melons are related to cucumbers: *Reticulatus* or netted melons, including muskmelons (sometimes called cantaloupes, though true cantaloupes are rarely seen) and Persian melons; and *Inodorus* or winter melons, including casabas, crenshaws, and honeydews. Watermelons belong to a different genus *(Citrullus)*. All three groups are hot weather plants, but you can grow them in less than ideal weather conditions if you give them special attention and don't mind taking a few risks.

We have dependable warm weather in April where we live. Must I start melons indoors?

Even if you live in a warm-climate area, you might want to start your melon vines indoors three to four weeks before the average date for the last frost. Plant seeds in peat pots, or other containers that can be set directly in the ground, for melons don't take well to having their roots disturbed at transplanting time.

When can melons be planted outdoors?

Transfer them to the garden once daytime temperatures regularly reach at least 60° F. You can set them out a little earlier if you put them under hot caps or cloches. Plastic milk jugs with their lids off and their bottoms cut out work well—but remember to remove them during the day if the sun shines hard or the plants might get burned.

How should I plant melon seeds?

Sow seeds 1 inch deep in hills (see page 73), two to four seeds per hill, 4 to 6 feet apart. Some bush varieties can be spaced closer together. If you plant melons in rows, space them according to package directions.

I don't have much space left in my garden. Can I train melons to climb a trellis?

Yes, and they look quite attractive grown this way. To be certain the fruits don't break off, or pull the vines from their supports, you may wish to create little "hammocks" for them with pieces of cloth or nylon stockings.

Ann Reilly

Muskmelons: When muskmelons are ripe, the stems will easily break away from the vines.

Can I grow melons in dry areas?

In dry areas, plant the seeds in depressions 3 to 5 inches deep. If you're transplanting seedlings, set them halfway up the sides of the depressions and train the plants away from the depressions so that they won't get muddy.

Can I grow watermelon in my area, where summers are cool?

If you live in a cooler climate, grow the smaller, "ice-box" watermelons. Search seed catalogues for varieties that can be grown in your area or seek advice from your Extension Service agent. Always reserve the warmest spot in your garden for melons. All melons, but particularly watermelons, need not only warm air both day and night, but warm soil as well. Keep down weeds that shade the soil and compete with the melons for water and nutrients. Use black plastic mulch to trap heat in the soil.

How much fertilizer do melons need?

Fertilize at planting or transplanting time (and water thoroughly without delay), again when the plants are well established and about to send out runners, and once again when the runners are 2 feet long. The best way to fertilize melons is to work the fertilizer into circular furrows 8 inches all the way around the plants.

Will I have to give melons extra water?

Melons need plenty of water, but they must also have good drainage. This is why they are usually planted in raised mounds. However, if water is in short supply where you live, planting them on the "walls" of a depression accomplishes the same effect. Drip irrigation systems under mulch are especially suited to melon culture.

How can I know when melons are ready to harvest?

For muskmelons, record your planting date, so that you know when to expect them to mature. When the melons look ripe, with your thumb apply a little pressure where the stem meets the fruit. If the stem easily breaks away, it is at the "full slip" stage and is ripe. If merely lifting up the melon separates it from the vine, it is "vine ripe," or even overripe. If the fruits smell melony, chances are they are ripe.

For watermelons, snap your fingertip or rap with your knuckle against the melon: If the sound is sharp and high, the melon is immature; if dull and hollow, it may be ripe. When the tendril, or curlicue, closest to the melon is alive and green, it is almost certainly immature. When it dies, the melon is ripe. Don't leave the melon on the vine longer than two weeks after the tendril dies. Another test is to watch for a yellowing of the spot where the melon rests on the ground. A ripe melon, when pressed with a bit of weight, will usually "crackle," but if you plan to store the melon, it is better not to push on it in this manner.

Mustard *(Brassica)*

What are mustard greens like?

Mustard greens are very easy to grow, and quite tender and flavorful when they are young. Chinese or Japanese mustard greens are much more subtle, extremely delicious, and less bitter than common mustard greens. Oftentimes they appear in catalogues simply as "greens" or "Oriental greens." Look for Tatsoi, Mizuna (delicious raw in salads), Purple Mustard, and Gai Choy.

How is mustard grown?

The seeds of this cool-weather *Brassica* should be thinly sown as early in the spring as the ground can be worked—¼ inch deep and ¾ inch apart in rows 12 to 14 inches apart. Thin the seedlings (and eat the thinnings) to whatever spacings are recommended for the variety you are growing. Mustard makes a good container plant because its roots are not extensive.

Are there any special tricks to keeping mustard from getting too bitter?

Keep mustard growing fast in good garden soil and it will develop its mildest, most subtle flavor. Hot spells may encourage it to bolt, so you probably won't have much luck starting succession crops after late May. It would be better to wait and plant in late summer for a fall harvest. Fertilize as you would for cabbage.

How is mustard harvested for greens?

Some varieties, such as Tatsoi, form a rather tight rosette, and are best harvested in their entirety. Others, such as Osaka Purple, may be picked a leaf at a time, which is all you need to spice up a salad. As long as you leave a few leaves on a mustard plant, it will keep growing for you as long as the weather stays cool and the ground stays moist. If you let mustard bolt to seed, it will produce a lovely show of yellow, sweet-smelling flowers. Don't let the seed pods mature, however, or you may have a weed problem in future years.

Are only the leaves and seeds of mustard edible?

All parts of Chinese mustard, including the root, are edible. The flowers make lovely additions to salads. Mustards are highly nutritious, abounding in calcium, vitamins C and A, and iron, as well as fiber.

Okra *(Abelmoschus)*

What is okra like?

This vegetable is unusual for its ability to thicken soups and stews, and it is also a favorite for pickling. Many East Indian curries call for okra. It has large, yellow flowers with red centers, borne on 4- to 5-foot-tall leafy bushes. Dwarf varieties grow 2 to 3 feet tall.

Can I grow okra in New England?

Yes, but the harvest will be brief. Okra loves hot weather and sunshine, and will not do well without them. If you live in a cool or cloudy area of the country, you may be able to grow okra by starting the seed indoors a month before setting it out. When there is no danger of frost, bring the plants outdoors to harden off (see page 71), and transplant seedlings to the warmest spot in your garden, away from any cool breezes.

How should I plant okra seed outdoors?

Soak the seed in water for twenty-four hours, and then plant it in good garden soil that has not been heavily fertilized, setting the seed ¼ inch deep in rows 24 to 30 inches apart. Later thin seedlings to stand 12 to 18 inches apart. You can also grow it three plants to a hill 3 feet across.

What are okra's water and fertilizer needs?

Okra stands up to droughty conditions, but don't let it get completely thirsty. Occasional deep waterings are best. Too much nitrogen makes the plants grow large and leafy without setting many pods. Make sure your soil contains plenty of phosphorus (found abundantly in bonemeal and rock phosphate).

How should I harvest okra?

Okra, like green beans, needs to be harvested at the immature stage. Continual picking of the pods when they are 3 inches long and not too thick across the middle will keep the plants producing. Large pods are pithy and tough.

Onions; Scallions; Shallots *(Allium)*

Are onions difficult to grow?

No matter where you live, there is at least one variety of onion that will thrive there. But because this vegetable is particular about the number of hours of light and darkness it gets as it grows, you must not only plant the appropriate variety for your area, but the right one for the time of year in which you grow it. It is particularly important to plant short-day types, such as Yellow Bermuda or Crystal Wax, if you live in the South and long-day types, such as Early Yellow Globe or Southport White Globe, if you live in the North.

How should I prepare the soil for onions?

Onions are heavy feeders and need well-limed, well-fertilized, heavy (but not sticky and wet) soil. Whether the soil is claylike or sandy, onions do best when lots of organic matter has been added to the soil. Work plenty of manure into the soil before you plant, and add a balanced fertilizer at the same time. Wood ashes are excellent for onions; sidedress liberally when the plants have put out a number of shoots.

Should I plant seeds or sets?

Grow onions from sets for summer use, or from seed for winter storage. Onions are also commonly transplanted from seedlings. Many gardeners feel that seed-grown onions are better than those grown from sets.

How are sets planted?

As soon as the soil can be made ready in the spring, push sets into prepared soil, so that their tops are about ½ inch below the surface. If you want to grow large onions, space the sets 3 to 4 inches apart; for scallions or bunching onions, space sets about 1 inch apart. Don't plan to thin out and use alternate onions for scallions, because this disturbs the roots of those left to form large bulbs.

How are onion seeds planted?

Indoors, sow seeds five to six weeks before planting time in the garden (a few days after the average last frost date), and transplant seedlings into the garden, spaced 4 inches apart in rows 12 to 15 inches apart. Snip just a little off the tops of the greens and the bottoms of the roots at transplanting time to encourage rapid growth. To begin seeds outdoors, as early in the spring as the ground can be worked, plant seed in rows 12 to 15 inches apart, with one to three seeds per inch, and cover them with ¼ inch of soil. Thin so that seedlings are 3 to 4 inches apart for large onions.

Why is it important to plant onions early in spring?

Onions need to grow big tops before the lengthening day triggers bulb formation. If the tops are still small when bulbs begin to form, the bulbs will be small. By getting onions into the soil as early in the spring as possible, you give them plenty of time to grow food-producing leaves that will feed the bulbs so they can grow big.

Ann Reilly

Onions: These heavy feeders need well-limed, well-fertilized soil.

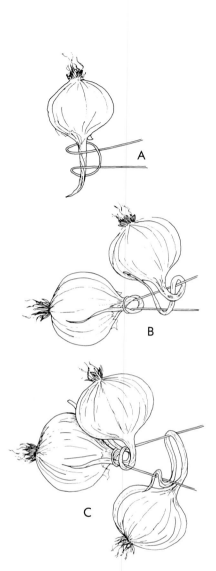

To braid onions, (A) loop string around onion top as shown, (B) braid in second onion, and (C) repeat with third onion and others.

What care should I give the growing plants?

Weed thoroughly early in the season, then mulch to thwart weeds. Onions are shallow rooted, and frequent hoeing would damage roots. Make sure to water during dry weather. The ground should never dry out below the surface. If flowers begin to form, break the flowering stalks so that they hang bent over. Don't break them all the way off, as they may collect water, which could rot the bulb.

When should onions be harvested?

Wait until the tops have fallen over and begun to brown, then pull up the onions and leave them to dry outside in the sun for a week or more. Be sure they have plenty of warmth and ventilation so that they dry completely. Remove the tops, and store the onions in a dry, dark, cool place. To make onion braids, leave the tops on some onions, and after they have dried, braid the tops together with a length of cord and hang them in a cool, dark place. Plant good storing onions if you intend to keep them for a long time. Spartan Sleeper, for example, will keep for up to six months at room temperature, but Walla Walla, a wonderfully sweet and juicy onion, should not be stored for any length of time.

Is it true that onions repel insects from other plants?

This seems to be the case, but keep onions away from your peas and beans, for these are not good onion companions.

What are scallions?

Several kinds of onions with long straight bulbs are used for scallions. You can harvest immature, seed-grown onions before they form bulbs and call them scallions, or you can grow perennial bunching onions, most commonly White Lisbon, although yellow and red varieties are also available. These form many small narrow bulbs, or stalks, rather than one fat one, as typical onions do. Once bunching onions are sown they will continue to divide on their own, dying back in cold winters and reappearing in spring, when they are best and mildest. You can also harvest immature shallots as scallions. When harvesting scallions from bunching onions, leave some behind so that they will continue to grow and divide.

Could you please describe shallots?

Shallots are as easy to grow as onions, especially when planted from sets. Each shallot plant separates into a number of bulbs, and the smaller ones are used as sets to grow new clusters of bulbs. Place them 1 inch deep, 6 inches apart, in rows 8 inches apart. Shallots are so hardy that you can plant sets in September for scallions during the winter.

How should I treat shallots when they are growing?

Tend to your shallot bed as you do your onion bed. Harvest them after their tops die down in the summer. Dry them in the sun for a few days, and then store them in a cool, dark, dry place.

Parsnips (Pastinaca)

When and how should I plant parsnip seeds?

Sow parsnips when you sow carrots. To hasten germination, soak seed overnight before planting. The seed takes two to three weeks to germinate under ideal conditions; keep the soil well moistened during this period. A thin mulch of organic material will help immensely. Set the seed ¼ inch deep, twelve seeds per foot, and cover it with sifted compost or leaf mold. Leave 18 to 24 inches between rows. Thin seedlings to stand 3 to 4 inches apart.

What kind of soil do parsnips need?

Since parsnip roots can easily reach 12 inches in length, they need deep, loose, well-drained soil, free from large rocks and chunks. Parsnips take up to four months to grow, and sometimes more. Don't give them too much nitrogen or they'll put their energy into growing lush tops rather than tasty roots. Phosphorus, responsible for strong stem and root development in plants, must be in good supply for parsnip crops. If the tops start to flower, break off the flower stalks.

When should I harvest parsnips?

The roots taste sweetest after the tops have been touched by a few fall frosts. Dig them up in the fall, or, if you live in a cold-winter area, leave them in the ground and dig them up in March—few things are more satisfying to a northern gardener than harvesting sweet parsnips from the soil at that bleak time of year. Store parsnips as you would carrots. In the refrigerator, they keep best in a plastic bag.

Peas (Legumes)

What are the differences between garden, snap, and snow peas?

Garden peas—or English peas as they are sometimes called—are available in both bush and climbing varieties. Although bush peas bear for a shorter period than pole beans, they don't require support. Unlike garden peas, both snap and snow peas have edible pods. Snap pea pods are sweet and crunchy; some varieties may also be shelled. Snow peas, common to Oriental cuisine, are harvested when still flat-podded.

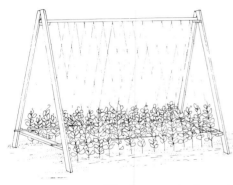

A permanent trellis for peas (or beans) can be constructed A-frame fashion, using 2x2s for uprights and top horizontal, and rebars for the bottom horizontals. String twine between top and bottom horizontals to support vines.

Climbing peas will readily climb a wire fence, netting, or trellis.

What is the best way to support peas?

You can buy netting made expressly for this purpose. Or use chicken wire stapled to stakes or twine strung between horizontal poles.

Can I grow peas in Louisiana?

You will have most success if you grow them as a fall crop. Peas are a cool-weather crop that can be grown just about anywhere, so long as you plant them at a time of year when sixty to seventy days of mild, cool weather are ahead.

How can I tell when peas are ready to harvest?

Garden peas are ready to pick when the pods are swollen and still shiny. Pick sugar pod peas once the pods have filled out but before the individual peas begin to show through in bumps. Snow peas taste best when they are about 3 inches long. While bush varieties of garden peas tend to ripen all at once, pole and snow peas produce over a longer period of time, and should be kept picked so that they will continue to produce. When you are done harvesting for the season, till the vines back into the soil for their value as a green manure.

Positive Images, Jerry Howard

Are peas prone to diseases?

In damp climates, mildew can be a problem if peas are planted so tightly that they lack ventilation. Dust with sulphur, and next time space your rows more generously. Crop rotation and the planting of resistant varieties are your best controls against disease.

Peppers (*Capsicum*)

Will peppers grow in cooler climates?

Both sweet and hot pepper varieties have been developed for cooler climates.

Should I start peppers indoors?

Yes. Start them eight to ten weeks before it will be safe to transplant them outdoors. Keep them in the warmest spot in your house (80° F. if possible) until they germinate; then move them to a sunny windowsill. Move them away from the window to a warmer spot at night if the weather outside is icy. Pepper seedlings are not as hardy as tomato seedlings. If you plant the seeds outdoors, it is essential to wait until the soil is warm. Sow four seeds per foot and thin to 12 to 18 inches apart in rows 2 to 3 feet apart.

How can I keep pepper seedlings from getting tall and spindly?

Move them to larger pots as they grow. When you set them out in the open, they should be bushy and compact. They may have some flower buds on them, but it is best if the buds are not yet open. Protect the seedlings from chilly winds with hot caps (see page 82).

Can I grow peppers in containers?

These plants thrive in containers and are one of the most ornamental annual vegetables you can grow. Given plenty of light in a sunny (but not intensely hot) window, they can even be grown indoors. If you grow them indoors, hand-pollinate them by moving from one flower to the next, gently brushing them with a soft-bristled brush, such as a makeup or artist's brush.

Last year I had beautiful foliage on my pepper plants, but the blossoms dropped before fruiting. What went wrong?

The ideal outdoor temperatures for peppers are between 70° and 80° F. during the day, and no lower than 60° F. at night. Smaller-fruited varieties withstand more variation in temperature than the larger-fruited. Some experts believe too much nitrogen causes blossom drop, but all experts agree that temperatures above 90° F. cause blossom drop, and insufficient calcium causes nutrient deficiency. To keep peppers cool, spray

Ann Reilly

Peppers: These Sweet Banana peppers have thick, sweet, mild flesh.

Ron West

Peppers: String bumper crops of hot peppers and hang them to ripen and dry in a warm, airy place.

them with water in the middle of a hot day. Keep them supplied with calcium by adding gypsum or lime to the soil before planting, and give sidedressings of chicken manure and dolomitic limestone right after blossom set, and every three weeks thereafter. Don't dig these materials in, because peppers have shallow, easily damaged roots. Hand-weed for the same reason. The first blossoms are likely to drop no matter what you do—don't worry about that.

When can I start picking peppers?

Pick the first peppers while they are green and rather small, to give the plants opportunity to set a good main crop. In long-season areas, peppers can be left on the bush to ripen to their expected color—dark green, yellow, orange, purple, chocolate, or red. String bumper crops of peppers and hang them to ripen and dry in a warm, airy place.

How can I avoid blossom-end rot?

Be sure plants are receiving adequate moisture and calcium.

Potatoes *(Solanum)*

Can you suggest some new varieties of potatoes to grow?

The selection of potato varieties now available is delightful— finger potatoes, yellow, red, and blue potatoes, enormous bakers, and diminutive salad potatoes. Look for yellow-fleshed Bintje and Yellow Finn potatoes and Ruby Crescent, a deep pink, fingerling type with yellow flesh.

Is it necessary to start potatoes from seed?

Though potatoes can be grown from seed, it is easier to purchase certified disease-free seed potatoes. Keep them in a cold place until you are ready to plant them.

What kind of soil and climate do potatoes need?

Potatoes prefer a sandy or clay loam, and do not do well in heavy clays. Acid soils are best, though not a must. Plant potatoes four to six weeks before the last frost date in your area. Potatoes need three to four months to mature. Potatoes can be grown in any region of the United States and Canada where other vegetables are grown. They are warm-weather plants but prefer fairly cool summers.

How do you prepare the seed potatoes for planting?

Cut 1½- to 2-inch chunks, each containing at least one eye, from the seed potatoes. Larger chunks are better than smaller, and small potatoes need not be cut at all. Let the chunks air-dry in a cool, dark, indoor spot for three to five days before planting.

To prepare seed potatoes for planting, cut them into 1 1/2- to 2-inch chunks, each containing at least one eye.

We have clay soil. We're working on improving it, but it is still very heavy. Is there any way we can grow potatoes?

Plant your potatoes on top of the soil if it's claylike or alkaline. Work the soil loose a foot or so down, and cover it with a 4-inch layer of straw or dry leaves. Lay pieces of seed potato on top of the mulch, and then cover them with another foot of straw or leaves. The potatoes will send roots into the soil and stems and leaves up through the mulch and into the air. New tubers will form in the mulch itself; they'll be easy to harvest and easy to clean. Potatoes grown this way rarely contract diseases. But the crop yield isn't as large as with in-ground potatoes.

How should I plant potatoes in the ground?

Three to five days before planting, dig a trench 1 foot wide and 6 inches deep, and work in some fertilizer and compost. Compost is particularly important because it helps the soil drain—if potatoes sit in water they are likely to rot. Don't use fresh

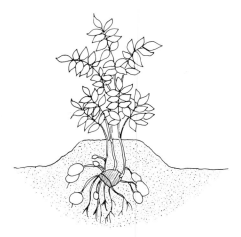

Hoe up soil around potato vines as they grow taller; potatoes grow underground on roots sent out from the seed potatoes.

manure, and do *not* lime the soil—potatoes prefer an acid pH. Set the potato chunks in furrows 3 inches deep, spacing them 6 to 12 inches apart. Closer spacings provide more, but smaller, potatoes. Water after planting.

How should I care for the potatoes while they are growing?

Hoe soil up around the vines as they grow taller, so that the tubers won't be exposed to light (which makes them turn green). This procedure also provides support to the vines and increases yields. A mulch of straw or dry leaves will help keep the ground cool and moist. Because potatoes have shallow roots, they need *regular* watering (about once a week) during dry weather. Alternate drought and wet causes potatoes to be rough and knobby.

How many potatoes will I get from a 50-foot row?

With a lot of compost and acid soil, you should be able to harvest about one bushel for every 50-feet.

When can I start harvesting potatoes?

Early potatoes—what a treat!—are ready to eat when they reach about golf-ball size. Let them sit in the refrigerator for a day before you eat them. To harvest full-grown tubers for storing, wait until the tops die down and then dig the entire crop. A potato fork is the best tool for this job. Dry your potato harvest in a dark, airy place for a few days before moving the tubers to a dark, quite cool place for long keeping.

Are potatoes likely to be attacked by disease?

Avoid diseases such as scab and late blight (the blight that caused the great Irish potato famine) by planting only certified seed potatoes, caring for your planting as described above, and rotating your crops on a three- to four-year basis.

I have heard that potatoes can be grown in containers. How is it done?

Simply plant them the same way you would in-ground potatoes, providing them with a deep container in which you can start the plants low and add a loose potting mix as the vines grow up. A trash can with drainage holes is not especially attractive, but will produce a surprisingly great number of potatoes. Keep the plants cool and moist.

Pumpkins. See Squash

Radicchio. See Chicory

Radishes *(Raphanus)*

When can I put radishes in?

Sow radish seeds as soon as the ground can be worked in the spring, and thereafter in succession until warm weather. Sow late crops in early fall.

How should I plant radishes?

Loosen the soil a foot down, work in plenty of compost, rake it smooth, and run a line of seed ½ inch deep and ½ to 1 inch apart in rows 8 to 12 inches apart. Or you can broadcast the seeds onto a seed bed before it is completely smooth, and then rake it flat. Tamp down the soil and water immediately. Thin radishes to stand 1 to 2 inches apart once the seedlings are an inch or so high. You can also mix radish seeds thinly with other vegetable seeds; the quick-sprouting radishes will break the soil for their tenderer companions and mark the rows for you.

Do radishes need any special care?

Water and weed regularly. Though radishes will grow no matter what, they must grow as quickly as possible in order to be sweet and tenderly crisp.

What is the Japanese Daikon radish like?

From 8 inches to 3 feet long, the Japanese Daikon tastes wonderful raw. It can also be pickled—it's beautiful in a tall jar with a small red pepper or two.

Rhubarb *(Rheum)*

Can I grow rhubarb in the South?

This hardy perennial is a cool-weather plant and most varieties need to be in frozen ground two months a year. If you live in a warm climate, be sure to buy a variety developed for warm weather.

How is rhubarb planted?

As early in the spring as you can work the ground, prepare the planting bed by digging in a good amount of compost. Soak rhubarb crowns in a bucket of water while you prepare the planting bed. Plant three or four crowns 2 inches below the surface of the soil, and space the groups 2 to 3 feet apart. Water immediately.

How much fertilizer and water should I give rhubarb?

Mulch with manure once a year to provide the modest amount of nitrogen that rhubarb needs. Keep rhubarb watered but not overly wet, and give it sun but not intense heat.

When can I begin harvesting rhubarb?

Harvest no stalks the first year. You can snap off a few stalks at the base the second year, but go lightly. Starting the third year you should be able to harvest all you need from the three or four crowns you planted. Do not eat the leaves—they contain oxalic acid in poisonous amounts.

Can I divide rhubarb?

Mature crowns can be dug up and separated to create new plants. Try growing some rhubarb in containers. It makes a handsome plant, with its thick, green leaves and lipstick-red stalks.

Roquette. See Arugula

Rutabaga. See Turnips

Scallions. See Onions

Shallots. See Onions

Spinach (*Spinacia*)

Every time I try to grow spinach it bolts. Why is this?

Spinach requires the hard-to-find weather combination of bright sun and cool air. Faced with any sort of stress, be it warm weather, inadequate moisture, or rapid temperature changes, it bolts to seed, turning bitter in the process. In spite of this, spinach is worth growing because of its nutritional value and exquisite flavor, both raw in salads and cooked as a pot herb. It needs rich soil and steady moisture in a sunny, weed-free bed.

If I get my seeds in early enough, will the spinach be less likely to bolt?

Get your spinach seeds in the ground just as early in the spring as you can, so that they will have time to grow up before warm spring weather causes them to bolt. In mild-winter areas, plant spinach from mid-January to March 1, and then again from August 1 to mid-November. In colder areas, plant it six to eight weeks before the last expected frost, and again four to six weeks before the first expected fall frost. Sow seeds ½ inch deep, 2 inches apart, in rows 12 to 18 inches apart; thin to 4 inches in the rows. Plant in succession every seven to ten days for a large, prolonged harvest.

How is spinach harvested?

You can begin harvesting outer leaves when they are egg-sized. If you wait until the plants are more mature, be sure to catch them before they bolt. Cut plants all the way down to an inch above the soil; they will come up again for a second shearing.

Will spinach be likely to have many pest and disease problems?

Spinach, fast grower that it is, is not terribly bothered by insects. Leaf miner is the worst pest: Destroy damaged plant leaves. Grow varieties that are tolerant to mosiac virus and downy mildew (blue mold).

I have seen New Zealand spinach advertised as being able to tolerate heat. Is that true?

New Zealand spinach, sometimes called summer spinach, is not spinach at all, but resembles it when cooked. Unlike true spinach, it loves heat and is very easy to grow, but it makes a slow start. Soak seed two or three days before planting; sow eight to ten seeds per foot in rows at least 2 feet apart; thin plants to about 8 inches. Although New Zealand spinach grows best in hot weather, it will sprout only in cool soil, so plant it early. This plant is a tremendous yielder, and an average family needs only a few feet of row.

Squash, summer and winter (Cucurbita)

When should I start squash seeds if I plant them indoors?

Three to four weeks before all danger of frost is past. When you transplant them into the garden, be especially careful not to disturb the roots. You can also sow seed directly into the soil, when all frost danger is past. You can plant summer squash in rows 4 to 5 feet apart, with seedlings 3 feet apart; or you can plant them in hills 4 to 6 feet apart, with each hill containing three plants, 6 inches apart. To accommodate sprawling vines, place winter squash hills farther apart, up to 8 feet. You can pinch off the growing tips of vines where you want them to stop. The soil must be at least 60° F. at planting time, but 70° F. is much better. Squash seed simply won't germinate in cold soil. If you dig in great quantities of manure and compost before planting, you'll get bigger fruits.

If you are planting in hills, smooth a flat, 1-foot in diameter circle on the prepared soil and evenly space six to nine seeds around the circle, gently pressing them into the soil with your fingertip to the required planting depth. Firm soil by tamping with your hand or a flat-bottomed tool such as a hoe.

What kind of care does squash require while it is growing?

Keep down weeds until the plants' leaves are big enough to shade them out. Water very deeply once a week if there is no rain, but avoid watering from above, as this invites disease. Stop watering winter squash once the vines start to die. Don't worry

Ann Reilly

Summer squash: Once plants begin to put out flowers, they produce fruit that ripens very rapidly, and plants should be harvested frequently to keep squashes from getting too large.

when the leaves of many squashes droop most forlornly in the midday sun—they will perk up later in the day. Provide a trellis for climbers such as tromboncino. Sidedress with a complete fertilizer before the plants get big.

When should I start harvesting summer squash?

Keep a close eye on the plants once they begin putting out flowers. Many of the flowers will probably be male flowers, so they won't all set fruit, but those that do will ripen very quickly. All summer squashes are far superior when they are quite small—six inches or less is the rule for zucchini. Harvest tromboncino at 8 to 18 inches. Those oversized specimens that hide behind leaves until they reach baseball bat size can be stuffed, or grated for zucchini bread.

Can you suggest some good summer squashes to try?

The fairly new Sunburst patty pan, an All-America winner, is as prolific as zucchini, and like the other patty pans is delicious. Scallopini, crookneck, Goldrush zucchini, and the tremendous Italian tromboncino, which puts out a 30- to 40-foot vine in one season, are all excellent summer squashes.

When should I harvest winter squash?

Leave winter squashes on their spent vines right up until just before the first hard frost. Avoid scratching or bruising the skin and leave a length of thoroughly dried stem on each squash to keep rot from entering at the scar while they are stored.

How should I store winter squash?

Store winter squash in a cool (45° to 50° F.), quite dry place. Some gardeners wipe the fruits with a light bleach and water solution before putting them away, to kill bacteria and fungi on the surface. Squashes keep best if they are set, with their sides not touching, on shelves. Check them regularly, and eat the ones that first show damage to their skins. Stored properly, the squashes may last you well into February or even longer.

Can you suggest a good variety of winter squash?

Perhaps the most delicious of all are the Japanese kabocha, or butterball, types. These smallish (3 to 4 pounds), light or dark green to flashy orange squashes taste as sweet as pumpkin pie when cut in half and baked face-down in a 350° F. oven until soft. They are prolific and about as easy to grow as anything you can plant.

Winter squash: Buttercup squashes like this Sweet Mama are sweet, easy to grow, and good storers.

Ann Reilly

Pumpkins: Miniature pumpkins make perfect fall decorations.

Is it true that squash flowers are edible?

Squash blossoms are a table delicacy that is often difficult to find in a market. Some varieties, such as Butterblossom, have been bred to put out great numbers of male blossoms. Costata Romanesco and Florina produce small fruits with the flowers still attached. Squash blossoms can be sautéed, deep-fried, stir-fried, stuffed with ricotta cheese and chives, and used in many other delicious ways. Picking the male flowers only does not hurt production.

What are some good pie pumpkins?

Select one of the smaller, "sugar pumpkin" varieties. Any sweet, orange-fleshed winter squash can be used for good pumpkin pie.

How can I grow extra large Jack-o-lanterns?

Plant three seeds to a hill, but thin to the one healthiest seedling. As soon as the fruits appear, remove all but two or three, or even one, of the young fruits, and pinch off extra vines. If you do this, all the plants' energy will be concentrated on these few pumpkins, which will grow quite large. In addition, side-dress the plants by putting fertilizer in circular trenches several feet out from the stem, two or three times during the season.

Can squashes be planted in containers?

Almost any bush variety of summer squash does splendidly in large patio containers, and varieties of acorn squashes that grow on compact bushes, such as Table King, can be grown in containers.

Sunflowers *(Helianthus)*

Why grow sunflowers in the garden?

The seeds of these enormous flowers are easy to harvest, they make fine snacks for humans, small animals, and birds; and, not least important, there is something spirit-lifting about a line of sunflowers at the edge of a garden.

How are sunflower seeds planted?

Sow sunflower seeds ½ inch deep and 6 inches apart after all danger of frost is past. When they are 3 inches high, thin them to 2-foot spacings.

Are sunflowers particular about where they grow?

Sunflowers thrive in the worst soil, and they don't need a lot of water. If your soil is good and nutrient-rich, you may have to stake the 12- to 14-foot sunflowers that spring out of it. Sunflower

Sunflowers: Seeds from a row of cheery sunflowers are excellent snacks for both people and birds.

stalks, cured in the sun and stored in a cool, dry place, make good bean poles. You can even grow some kinds of pole beans on live sunflower stalks, if you strip enough of the flowers' lower leaves to let the sun get to the beans.

How should I harvest sunflowers?

Cut the heads from the stalks when the seeds are fully mature. Rub two heads together or, better still, rub the heads on a piece of ½-inch hardware cloth stretched over a wooden frame. Cure the seeds in a very dry and airy place for a week, and then store them in sealed jars or other airtight containers. For next year's planting, save some seed in a cool, dry place.

Are sunflowers hard to grow?

Birds may harvest your sunflower seeds before you do. If you don't want them to, tie nylon screen or netting over the heads before the seeds mature. Insects and disease don't bother sunflowers.

Sweet potatoes *(Ipomoea)*

Is it possible to grow sweet potatoes only in the South? I'd love to be able to grow them here in Vermont.

Although sweet potatoes, which are also called yams, are grown commercially only in the hottest states, home gardeners grow them in much cooler places—even in Vermont. The secret

133

is to plant slips (small plants sprouted from slices of sweet potatoes) at the correct time, and to protect the young plants on cold nights.

When should I get sweet potatoes in the ground?

Sweet potatoes go in the ground in late spring, when the soil has thoroughly warmed. Order certified disease-free slips from a mail-order house (be sure they will arrive as close to planting time as possible), and plant them 3 inches deep, 10 to 12 inches apart, in raised beds 3 to 4 feet apart.

What kind of soil should sweet potatoes be planted in?

Enrich your soil with compost, well-aged manure, or other organic matter two weeks before you plant. Sweet potatoes do not fare well in heavy clay soil. They need nitrogen, but not too much. If you buy a commercial preparation, use 5-10-10.

Do sweet potatoes need much care?

Weed regularly until the vines have grown big enough to take care of themselves. While the plants are still young, protect them during cold nights with a thick straw mulch. A sidedressing of 5-10-10—about 2 teaspoons per plant—is helpful once the plants have established themselves, but don't use too much. The vines will ramble, but don't injure them by pruning. Instead, loosen the soil where the stems are rooting at the joints.

How will I know when my sweet potatoes are ready for harvest?

Get your sweet potatoes out of the ground before the first fall frost—don't wait until the tops die down, as you would for Irish potatoes. If a light frost is possible, mulch the tops at night with a thick layer of straw or dried leaves. The potatoes should be mature four to five months after setting them out. If the first frost comes along before that and you have to dig up your crop early, the potatoes won't be "unripe," just a bit smaller than average. Sweet potatoes spread out farther from the parent plant than do Irish potatoes. Because they break easily, dig them up carefully, starting from a few feet to the outside of the plants, rather than right on top of them. Leave the potatoes on a dry patch of ground for just a few hours to dry in the sun, then keep them in a humid spot with a temperature of 70° to 80° F. to cure for two to three weeks. Long-time storage should be at 50° to 60° F. Avoid handling them while in storage, and eat bruised ones first. Don't wash sweet potatoes until you are ready to cook them.

Do sweet potatoes have any potential problems?

To avoid root-knot nematode infestations, do not plant sweet potatoes in a bed recently converted from sod. Sweet potatoes are robust growers, not affected greatly by insects or disease.

Swiss chard *(Beta)*

Is Swiss chard related to beets? The leaves look and taste somewhat alike.

Swiss chard (or just "chard") is a bulbless beet grown for its leaves and stems. Apart from being delicious, especially when steamed and eaten with butter and lemon juice, chard is a garden favorite because it is so easy to grow. The green and red leaf varieties are equally tasty.

Does Swiss chard have to be started indoors?

No. Sow seeds directly in the ground as early as the soil can be worked in the spring. In warmer climates, chard is also sown in the fall for harvests all winter long. You don't have to succession-crop chard because one patch, picked leaf by leaf, will keep you in greens indefinitely.

How far apart should chard seed be planted?

Sow the seed, which is grouped in clumps like beet seed, ½ inch deep, 4 inches apart, in rows 2 feet apart. Thin to 8-inch spacings in the rows.

Does chard need special care?

Chard will flourish in any good garden soil. If you let it reseed itself from year to year, the patch will have to be fertilized now and then with plenty of compost, manure, or a balanced commercial fertilizer. Chard will continue to produce, even during a drought. It is troubled by few pests and diseases.

Is it better to pull up whole plants, or harvest chard leaf by leaf?

Cut the outer leaves at the base, rather than pulling up the plant by the roots. You can cut the inner leaves, too, if you like the small, tender ones. The plants will take longer to come back this way, but come back they will.

Ann Reilly

Swiss chard: Easy-to-grow Swiss chard is prolific and delicious.

Tomatoes *(Lycopersicon)*

Is it true that tomatoes were once considered poisonous?

It is true, but they are now the most commonly grown home-garden vegetable. Seed catalogues offer innumerable varieties of tomatoes adapted to many climates and cultural conditions. The tomato is ideally suited to container growing, too, and can be trained to grow up, down, and around almost any trellis you provide it with.

I have seen tomatoes designated determinate and indeterminate. What do these terms mean?

Catalogue and seed-packet descriptions usually note whether a tomato variety is determinate or indeterminate. The vines of determinate types do not grow endlessly, but confine themselves to a fairly compact bush shape. Some gardeners stake them for extra support. They make good container and small-garden plants. The vines of indeterminate varieties continue to grow at their tips, and most gardeners provide support for them. They produce larger fruits over a longer period of time, but come into production later than determinate types.

Should I start my own seedlings or purchase nursery-grown ones?

Growing your own seedlings allows for a much wider choice of varieties. With care, you should be able to grow better plants at home than you sometimes find for sale—and they are on hand when planting conditions are just right. It is easier to buy plants, but if you need more than a few, the cost becomes significant. If you buy seedlings, choose those that are short and stout, and without fruit or, if possible, without flowers. Check to be sure that they are free of insects.

Tomatoes: Sun-ripened tomatoes have no match among the greenhouse varieties, and are the top favorite vegetable for gardeners to grow.

Positive Images, Jerry Howard

Can you please describe how to start seeds indoors?

Plant seeds in pots, peat pellets, or divided flats six weeks before the date of your last expected spring frost. Keep the soil warm, from 75° to 89° F., with the heat preferably coming from below. A heat mat is ideal, but the top of a radiator, water heater, or even the refrigerator will do the trick. Transplant the seedlings to 4-inch pots when the second set of leaves appears. Use potting soil when you transplant. If the leaves discolor, fertilize with fish emulsion or a diluted, liquid, complete fertilizer (according to label instructions). When you are sure there will be no more frosts, and nighttime temperatures go no lower than 45° F. (or better yet, 50° F.), take the plants outdoors to harden off for about a week before they are transplanted into the ground (see page 71).

How should I transplant tomatoes?

After hardening off, plant tomatoes as shown in the illustration on this page. For each plant, add 1 teaspoon of rock phosphate or 2 teaspoons of bonemeal at transplanting time, to supply the extra phosphorus tomatoes need. Or mix 2 teaspoons of 5-10-10 fertilizer in each planting hole, cover it with an inch of soil or compost, and plant the seedlings on top of that. Protect each plant with a cutworm collar (see page 86). Water thoroughly, and continue to water every two or three days, or every day in hot weather, for a week. It is best to transplant in the evening or on a cloudy day. If it is windy or cold, protect the seedlings with some kind of enclosure.

If you set tomato cages (see next question) in place at transplanting time, they can serve as frames to wrap plastic sheeting around. Cover the tops at night with paper, cardboard, or cloth (never plastic). Once the weather has fully warmed, the plants will outgrow their protective devices and do quite well on their own.

Should I use stakes or wire cages to support my tomatoes?

Wire cages have advantages over stakes: The cages reduce the risk of sunscald, which can be caused when fruits are totally exposed to the sun's rays without sufficient leaf covering; and the plants' side branches grow through the wire mesh and become self-supporting. In drought years, plants will lose less moisture to the wind if they are allowed to sprawl over a hay mulch, but generally, unsupported fruit is subject to rotting and greater insect damage. Tomatoes may also be trained up a trellis.

Will I have to give tomatoes a lot of extra water?

During dry weather, water occasionally but deeply, from below rather than above, if possible. Mulch heavily with straw, shredded leaves, or some other dry organic material to retain moisture, but don't apply this mulch until the weather is warm, or you will cause the soil to be too cool.

Maggie Oster

Tomato cages reduce the risk of sunscald, provide carefree support for fast-growing plants, and lessen the incidence of pest and disease problems.

Do I have to prune tomatoes?

Pruning is not necessary except in short-season areas, where indeterminate types may not bear soon enough before the fall frosts. To prune, remove suckers from the vine crotches about once a week, when the plants are past the seedling stage. One or two suckers left low on the main stem of each plant will produce alternate main stems, making the plant fuller and reducing the likelihood of split fruits.

Do tomatoes need much fertilizing?

Once the fruit appears, sidedress with a complete fertilizer, following package instructions. A number of reliable fertilizers especially formulated for tomatoes are available through catalogues or in nurseries and garden centers. Avoid applying too much nitrogen, or the tomatoes may grow a lot of foliage at the expense of abundant fruit.

Why are my tomatoes producing flowers that drop off instead of developing fruits?

Blossom drop is caused most often by night temperatures below 55° or above 75° F. Perhaps you are growing a variety not well suited to your climate.

My tomatoes were high in quality but stopped fruiting by late July. What did I do wrong?

You planted a determinate variety, which sends up a limited number of growing stems, then stops growing vegetatively (stems and leaves) and produces fruits. While determinate varieties are early and heavy fruiting, their period of production is usually short.

My tomatoes went all to foliage. Why?

This may be due to too much shade (perhaps from spacing the plants too closely), or too much nitrogen in the soil. A fertilizer high in phosphorus, especially when applied at the time of flowering, will encourage heavier fruit yields and early ripening.

Why do tomatoes get black spots at the blossom end?

Blossom end rot comes from inadequate or irregularly supplied water. Regular irrigation will solve the problem. Also, add calcium, in the form of rock powders, to your soil.

Our summers are not cold, but the skies are overcast almost every day. Can we still grow tomatoes?

You will have difficulty ripening them, because tomatoes need at least six hours of sunlight each day. Grow a northern variety such as Sub-Arctic Maxi, Rocket, or Scotia, and bring the fruits indoors to ripen in a cool, dark place. Experiment with plantings

Ann Reilly

One or two cherry tomato plants produce a great quantity of fruit over a long period of time, and they provide a cheery decorative accent as well.

of several varieties recommended for areas with low amounts of sunshine (ask your county Extension Service agent).

Our tomatoes got big this year, but they never turned dark red. What happened?

Perhaps they suffered from sunscald, which happens when temperatures reach the nineties, or when intense sunlight shines directly on the fruit. Varieties resistant to sunscald bear large leaves that hide the fruit. Use tomato cages.

During the season pick your tomatoes as they ripen. If a fall frost is approaching, pull up the entire plants and hang them upside-down in a sheltered place, such as a garage, where they'll ripen in time. You can also ripen green tomatoes by putting them in a paper bag with an apple.

What pests and diseases bother tomatoes?

The most common tomato pests are aphids, flea beetles, Colorado potato beetles, hornworms, cutworms, and whiteflies. See pages 86-87 for controls. Of diseases, early blight is one of the most common, especially among early, determinate varieties. It appears as brown spots ringed by an expanding circle, which spreads from the lower to the upper leaves. To avoid it, lay an organic mulch around your plants, and water from below rather than above. Practice clean garden sanitation, including the removal of weeds and fall crop residues. Leaf spot can be controlled by crop rotation. If fusarium and verticillium wilts are a problem in your area, plant resistant varieties. Nematode deterrence is also bred into some plants. Tobacco mosaic can be prevented by never smoking near tomato plants, never handling tomato plants with unwashed hands after you have smoked, and never planting tobacco nearby.

Turnips; Rutabagas *(Brassica)*

What is the difference between turnips and rutabagas?

Turnips are a hardy root crop with tasty and highly nutritious greens; rutabagas (also called Swedes) are their cousins, and are more reliable keepers than turnips for winter storage. Although turnips are usually white-fleshed and rutabagas yellow-fleshed, there are yellow turnips and white rutabagas. Turnips bear the more tender greens of the two. The roots of raw turnips and rutabagas make crisp, flavorful additions to salads, both contribute a full, sweet flavor to soups and stews, and both are also delicious boiled or steamed, mashed, and served with butter.

When should I plant turnips?

Turnips grow faster than rutabagas, and can be seeded in early spring to mid-spring and again in late summer and early fall.

Frost doesn't bother them. Rutabagas take from ninety to over one hundred days to mature, depending on the variety and cultural conditions, and in colder regions they are usually planted in late spring to midsummer for a fall harvest and winter storage. In warmer areas they are planted in early spring and in early to late fall. Sow the seeds of each directly in the ground, ½ inch deep and 1 inch apart in rows 1 foot apart. Thin so that plants stand 4 to 6 inches apart. The thinnings are tasty eaten raw or steamed.

What can I do to provide the best growing environment for turnips?

Try to keep both turnips and rutabagas growing steadily, but not fast. They will do best in slightly alkaline soil (add lime if your soil is at all acid). The soil should be moist and low in nitrogen but enriched with potassium—apply 2 pounds of wood ashes, greensand, or granite dust per 100 feet of row to alleviate excess nitrogen.

How will I know when turnips are ready to be harvested?

Harvest both turnips and rutabagas on or before their maturity dates, as roots that grow too big will become tough. This is especially true for turnips. Harvest rutabagas for storage after they have been hit by a few frosts. Store them as you would carrots, in very cold, wet sand or sawdust (see page 103).

Glossary

BACILLUS POPILLIA. Milky spore disease, a bacterium that infects Japanese beetles.

BACILLUS THURINGIENSIS (Bt). A bacterium that causes disease in a variety of pest larvae, but is safe to humans, birds and pets, and plants; marketed under such tradenames as Biotrol, Dipel, and Thuricide.

BALLED-AND-BURLAPPED. A plant that has been dug up with the soil carefully maintained around its roots and wrapped in burlap (or plastic-backed burlap).

BARE-ROOTED. A plant that has been dug from its growing place and is usually shipped or sold wrapped in cardboard or plastic with roots protected with something like damp sphagnum moss.

BOLT. Premature formation of flowers and seed.

BORDEAUX MIXTURE. A fungicide made by combining copper sulfate, lime, and water.

BROADCAST. Scatter seeds freely over the entire seedbed.

CENTRAL-LEADER TRAINING. A method of pruning whereby a single trunk continues up the center of the tree, with all scaffold branches emanating from it.

CHILLING REQUIREMENT. A dormant period of a specified period of time needed by many fruit trees, measured in hours when temperatures range between 32° and 45°F.

CLAY SOIL. A soil containing from 30- to 100-percent clay; fine-textured and sticky when wet.

COMPOST. A rich, porous mixture composed of decaying or decayed organic matter.

CONTAINER-GROWN. A plant that has been grown in some kind of pot for most or all of its life.

COTYLEDONS. The first, or seed leaves; food storage cells, not true leaves.

COVER CROP. Sown toward the close of the growing season to cover the ground until the following spring, a cover crop controls weeds, protects soil against erosion, and improves the nutrient content and texture of the soil. *See also* Green manure

CULTIVAR. A cultivated variety, usually unique and an improvement in the species, created by the successful cross-pollination of two different plants within a species.

DAMPING OFF. A fungus disease carried in unsterile soil; causes young seedlings to wither and die.

DORMANCY. A period of time during which plant growth and other activity ceases temporarily because of unfavorable weather.

DORMANT OIL. A refined petroleum product especially marketed for use on plants; listed as ''60'' or ''70 sec,'' the numbers referring to a viscosity rating (the lower the number the thinner the oil).

DRILL. A shallow furrow into which seed is sown.

DWARF TREE. A tree created by grafting a different variety onto rootstock that grows a tree less than a quarter of the diameter of a standard tree; fruit is standard sized.

EXTENSION SERVICE. The educational arm of the U.S. Department of Agriculture; there is a branch in every county in the country, often affiliated with the state university.

FLAT. A shallow, topless box with drainage holes in the bottom; used for germinating seeds, growing young transplants, or propagating cuttings.

GENETIC DWARF TREE. Developed through breeding rather than by grafting (*See* Dwarf tree), genetic dwarf trees are even smaller than dwarf trees.

GERMINATION. The sprouting of seeds.

GREEN MANURE. A cover crop that is grown to improve nitrogen availability in the soil and, when it is turned into the soil, to add humus to the soil. *See also* Cover crop

HARDENING OFF. The process of subjecting seedlings that were begun indoors to increasing amounts of light and outdoor temperatures prior to transplanting them into the garden.

HARDINESS ZONES. U.S. Department of Agriculture classifications according to annual minimum temperatures and/or lengths of growing seasons. *See* zone map, page 149.

HEELING IN. A technique whereby plants that cannot be immediately planted are lain on their sides in a shallow trench, with their roots covered with about 6 inches of soil.

HOT CAP. A plastic or paper tent made to protect young plants from wind and cold.

HUMUS. The brown substance that results following the breakdown of organic materials by various soil organisms.

HYBRID. A new plant created by the successful cross-pollination of two plants of two different species, thus with different genetic traits.

INSECTICIDAL SOAP. A specially prepared, biodegradable soap made from natural fatty substances that kills many insects on contact without damaging plants or harming people, animals, or beneficial insects.

KITCHEN GARDEN. A fairly small garden composed of edible plants, both vegetable and herb.

LEAF MOLD. Decayed leaves.

LOAM. A soil consisting of about a 50-50 mixture of sand and clay.

MICROCLIMATE. The average temperatures and other climatic conditions of a limited area, sometimes varying from the general climate of the wider region.

MODIFIED-LEADER TRAINING. A method of pruning whereby a single trunk is allowed to run a few feet higher than the trunk of an open-center-trained tree, and then to branch out.

MULCH. A protective covering, such as bark chips or sawdust, spread over the ground to reduce evaporation, maintain an even soil temperature, prevent erosion, control weeds, and enrich the soil.

NPK. Chemical symbols representing nitrogen, phosphorus, and potassium, respectively; the primary ingredients in most lawn and garden fertilizers.

NITROGEN. One of the three most important plant nutrients, an essential element of chlorophyll; stunted growth and pale yellow foliage indicate nitrogen deficiency. *See also* Phosphorus; Potassium

OPEN-CENTER TRAINING. A method of pruning whereby the center branches of a tree are kept pruned out, encouraging a vase-shaped tree.

PEAT MOSS. Compacted plant debris, including sphagnum moss.

pH. The relative acidity and alkalinity of a soil on a scale of 1 to 14; a soil with a pH of 7 is considered neutral.

PHEROMONE TRAPS. A trap consisting of synthesized versions of the odors naturally released by insects and animals to attract one another or communicate danger or food sources.

PHOSPHORUS. One of the three most important plant nutrients, essential for good root and stem development; stunted growth and purple coloring of leaves and stems indicate phosphorus deficiency. *See also* Nitrogen; Potassium

POLLINATION. The transfer of pollen from one flower (cross-pollination), or part of a flower (self-pollination), to another; a critical step in plant fertilization.

POTASSIUM. One of the three most important plant nutrients; slow growth, high incidence of disease, and bronzing of leaves indicate potassium deficiency. *See also* Nitrogen; Phosphorus

PRUNING. The process of removing dead, diseased, or unwanted parts of a tree so that those parts that remain are benefited.

ROTOTILL. To operate a rotary tiller.

SANDY SOIL. A soil with from 50- to 100-percent fine sands, as well as coarse sands with 35- to 100-percent fine gravel and some fine sand. Although sandy soil can be formed into a ball when wet, the ball will break easily when touched.

SCAFFOLD BRANCHES. Side branches.

SEEDLING. A young plant grown from seed.

SELF-FRUITFUL. Capable of maturing fruit by self-pollination.

SELF-STERILE. A plant that requires cross-pollination in order to bear fruit.

SLOW-RELEASE FERTILIZER. A fertilizer formulated to be inactive until released by water or temperature and to activate slowly over a period of time (e.g., 3-month or 6-month formulations).

SOIL AMENDMENTS. Ingredients such as sand, peat moss, or compost that are added to soil to improve its texture.

SOIL TEST. A measurement of the nitrogen/phosphorus/potassium, trace elements, minerals, salts, and pH levels of the soil. Gardeners can test their own soil with soil testing kits, or send soil samples to Extension Services.

SPECIES. The basic division of the living world, consisting of distinct and similar individuals that can breed together to produce offspring similar to themselves.

SUCCESSION PLANTING. Sowing seeds of a specific plant every one to two weeks over a period of time in order to have a continuous supply.

SUPERPHOSPHATE. A soluble mixture of phosphates used as a fertilizer; made by treating insoluble phosphates with sulfuric acid.

TAMPER. A tool similar to a mason's float; used for tamping soil firmly in flats when sowing seed.

TILL. To work the soil by cultivating or digging it.

TOPSOIL. The surface layer of soil, consisting of good loam and organic matter.

TRUE LEAVES. Those leaves that appear after the cotyledons, or seed leaves.

VARIETY. A plant that is different from the true species occurring in nature.

VASE TRAINING. *See* Open-center training

WINTER HARDY. Able to withstand frost.

Appendix

W. F. Allen Co.
P.O. Box 1577
Salisbury, MD 21801
Berries
Free catalog

Burgess Seed and Plant Co.
905 Four Seasons Rd.
Bloomington, IN 61701
Fruits and berries
Free catalog

W. Atlee Burpee Co.
300 Park Ave.
Warminster, PA 18991
Fruits and berries
Free catalog

C & O Nursery Co.
P.O. Box 116
Wenatchee, WA 98807
Fruits
Free catalog

California Nursery Co.
Niles District Box 2278
Freemont, CA 94536
Fruits and berries
Free price list

Cumberland Valley
  Nurseries
P.O. Box 471
McMinnville, TN 37110
Fruits
Free catalog

Farmer Seed and Nursery Co.
Dept. 77 Reservation Center
2207 East Oakland Ave.
Bloomington, IL 61701
Fruits and berries
Free catalog

Henry Field Seed &
  Nursery
Shenandoah, IA 51602
Fruits and berries
Free catalog

Fowler Nurseries, Inc.
Garden Center
525 Fowler Rd.
Newcastle, CA 95658
Fruits and berries
Free price list

Louis Gerardi Nursery
Garden Center & Gift Shop
1700 E. Highway 50
O'Fallon, IL 62269
Fruits and berries
SASE for free price list

Gurney's Seed and Nursery Co.
2nd and Capitol
Yankton, SD 57079
Fruits and berries
Free catalog

J. W. Jung Seed Co.
335 S. High St.
Randolph, WI 53957
Fruits and berries
Free catalog

Kelly Nurseries
19 Maple St.
Dansville, NY 14437
Fruits and berries
Free catalog

Lakeland Nursery Sales
Unique Merchandise Mart,
     Building 4
Hanover, PA 17333
Fruits and berries
Catalog, $1

Henry Leuthardt Nurseries
Montauk Hwy., Box 666
East Moriches, L.I., NY 11940
Fruits and berries
Free price list

J. E. Miller Nurseries, Inc.
5060 W. Lake Rd.
Canandaigua, NY 14424
Fruits and berries
Free catalog

New York State Fruit Testing
P.O. Box 462, North St.
Geneva, NY 14456
Fruits and berries
Free catalog

Rayner Bros, Inc.
P.O. Box 1617
Salisbury, MD 21801
Fruits and berries
Free catalog

Savage Farms Nurseries
P.O. Box 125
McMinnville, TN 37110
Fruits and berries
Free catalog

R. H. Shumway, Seedsman
P.O. Box 1
Graniteville, SC 29829
Fruits and berries
Catalog, $1, refundable
     with first order

Southmeadow Fruit Gardens
Box SM
Lakeside, MI 49116
Fruits and berries
Free price list

Spring Hill Nurseries
6523 N. Galena Rd.
Peoria, IL 61632
Berries
Free catalog

Stark Brothers
Hwy. 54
Louisiana, MO 63353
Fruits and berries
Free catalog

Van Well Nursery
P.O. Box 1339
Wenatchee, WA 98801
Fruits and berries
Catalog, $1

Waynesboro Nurseries
P.O. Box 987
Waynesboro, VA 22980
Fruits and berries
Free catalog

Burgess Seed and Plant Co.
905 Four Seasons Rd.
Bloomington, IN 61701
Catalog, $1

W. Atlee Burpee Co.
300 Park Ave.
Warminster, PA 18991
Free catalog

Comstock, Ferry & Co.
263 Main St.
Wethersfield, CT 06109
Free catalog

The Cook's Garden
Box 65
Londonderry, VT 05148
Catalog, $1

DeGiorgi Co., Inc.
P.O. Box 413
Council Bluffs, IA 51502
Catalog, $1

Farmer Seed and Nursery Co.
Dept. 77
Reservation Center
2207 East Oakland Ave.
Bloomington, IL 61701
Free catalog

Henry Field's Seed &
  Nursery Co.
Shenandoah, IA 51602
Free catalog

Gurney's Seed & Nursery Co.
2nd and Capitol
Yankton, SD 57079
Free catalog

Harris Seeds
961 Lyell Ave.
Rochester, NY 14606
Free catalog

Hastings, Seedsman to the South
P.O. Box 115535
Atlanta, GA 30310
Free catalog

J. L. Hudson, Seedsman
P.O. Box 1058
Redwood City, CA 94064
Catalog, $1

Johnny's Selected Seeds
305 Foss Hill Rd.
Albion, ME 04910
Free catalog

Le Jardin du Gourmet
West Danville, VT 05873
Catalog, $.50

Liberty Seed Co.
P.O. Box 806
New Philadelphia, OH 44663
Free catalog

Earl May Seed & Nursery Co.
Shenandoah, IA 51603
Free catalog

Nichols Garden Nursery, Inc.
1190 N. Pacific Hwy.
Albany, OR 97321
Free catalog

George W. Park Seed Co.
Cokesbury Rd.
Greenwood, SC 29647
Free catalog

Pinetree Garden Seeds
Route 100
New Gloucester, ME 04260
Free catalog

Redwood City Seed Co.
P.O. Box 361
Redwood City, CA 94064
Catalog, $1

Seeds Blum
Idaho City Stage
Boise, ID 83706
Catalog, $2

Seed Savers Exchange
Box 70
Decorah, IA 52101
Membership, $12

R. H. Shumway Seedsman
P.O. Box 1
Graniteville, SC 29829
Catalog, $1, refundable
  with first order

SUPPLIERS OF VEGETABLE SEEDS

Stokes Seeds, Inc.
Box 548
Buffalo, NY 14240
Free catalog

Thompson & Morgan
Box 1308
Jackson, NJ 08527
Free catalog

Otis Twilley Seed Co.
P.O. Box 65
Trevose, PA 19047
Free catalog

Vermont Bean Seed Co.
Garden Lane
Fair Haven, VT 05743
Free catalog

Vesey's Seeds, Ltd.
P.O. Box 9000
Houlton, ME 04730
   or
Prince Edward Island,
C0A 1P0, Canada
Free catalog

FURTHER READING

Crockett, James U. *Crockett's Victory Garden*. Little, Brown & Co., 1977.

Foster, Catharine Osgood. *Building Healthy Gardens: A Safe and Natural Approach*. Garden Way Publishing, 1989.

Gessert, Kate Rogers. *The Beautiful Food Garden*. Garden Way Publishing, 1987.

Gilbertie, Sal. *Home Gardening at Its Best*. Atheneum, 1977.

Hill, Lewis. *Cold-Climate Gardening: How to Extend Your Growing Season by at Least 30 Days*. Garden Way Publishing, 1987.

Fruits and Berries for the Home Garden. Garden Way Publishing, 1977.

Pruning Simplified. Garden Way Publishing, 1986.

Home Vegetable Garden. Brooklyn Botanic, n.d.

Page, Stephen, and Joe Smillie. *The Orchard Almanac: A Spraysaver Guide*. Spraysaver Publications, 1986.

Philbrick, Helen, and John Philbrick. *The Bug Book: Harmless Insect Controls*. Garden Way Publishing, 1974.

Raymond, Dick. *Down-to-Earth Vegetable Gardening Know-How*. Garden Way Publishing, 1975.

Garden Way's Joy of Gardening. Garden Way Publishing, 1982.

Riotte, Louise. *Carrots Love Tomatoes*. Garden Way Publishing, 1975.

Taylor's Guide to Vegetables & Herbs. Houghton Mifflin Co., 1987.

Tilgner, Linda. *Tips for the Lazy Gardener*. Garden Way Publishing, 1985.

Yepsen, Roger B., Jr. *The Encyclopedia of Natural Insect & Disease Control*. Rodale Press, 1984.

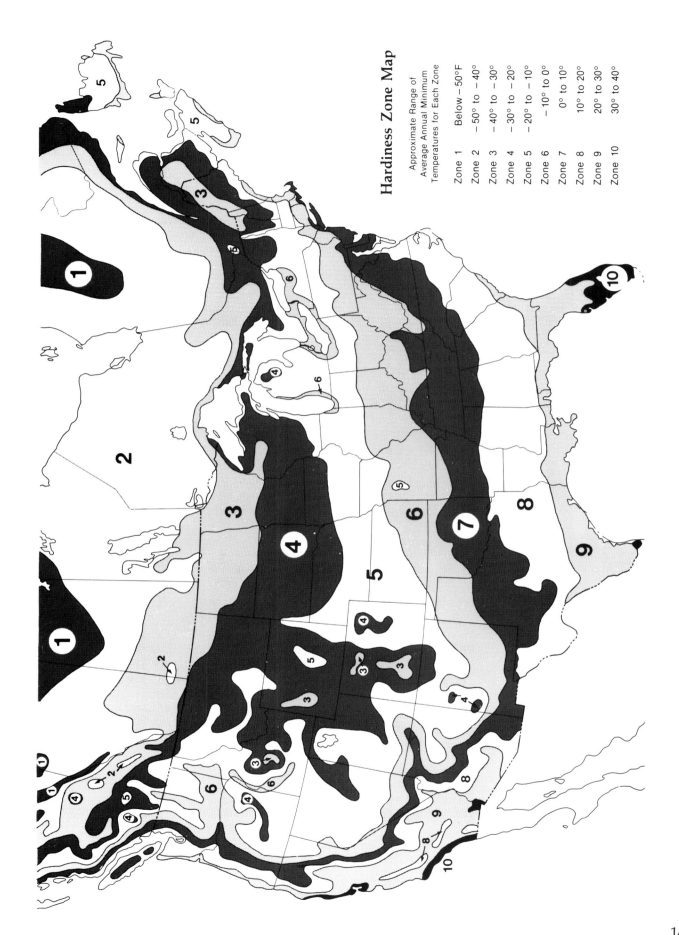

Hardiness Zone Map

Approximate Range of
Average Annual Minimum
Temperatures for Each Zone

Zone 1   Below −50°F
Zone 2   −50° to −40°
Zone 3   −40° to −30°
Zone 4   −30° to −20°
Zone 5   −20° to −10°
Zone 6   −10° to 0°
Zone 7   0° to 10°
Zone 8   10° to 20°
Zone 9   20° to 30°
Zone 10   30° to 40°

Index